MAY 1 9 2011

Raiten-D'Antonio, Toni, 1955-
    Ugly as sin

306.4613 RAITEN- D ANTONIO

D0560810

Boone County Library
Harrison, Arkansas

In Honor of

Polly Hudson

Friends of the Library
Honor Book Project 2011

WITHDRAWN

Property of the
Boone County Library
Harrison, AR

UGLY
AS
SIN

Toni Raiten-D'Antonio, LCSW

Author of *The Velveteen Principles* and *The Velveteen Principles for Women*

UGLY
AS
SIN

The Truth About How We Look and Finding Freedom from Self-Hatred

Health Communications, Inc.
Deerfield Beach, Florida

www.hcibooks.com

Please note—The names and identifying characteristics of therapy clients and some others mentioned in this text have been changed to protect their privacy.

Library of Congress Cataloging-in-Publication Data

Raiten-D'Antonio, Toni, 1955-
    Ugly as sin : the truth about how we look and finding freedom
from self-hatred / Toni Raiten-D'Antonio.
        p. cm.
    ISBN-13: 978-0-7573-1465-0
    ISBN-10: 0-7573-1465-1
    1. Self-acceptance.   2. Beauty, Personal.   3. Ugliness.
4. Body image.   I. Title.
BF575.S37R35 2010
306.4'613—dc22

                                                                    2010024018

© 2010 Toni Raiten-D'Antonio

All rights reserved. Printed in the United States of America. No part of this publication may be reproduced, stored in a retrieval system, or transmitted in any form or by any means, electronic, mechanical, photocopying, recording, or otherwise, without the written permission of the publisher.

HCI, its logos, and marks are trademarks of Health Communications, Inc.

Publisher: Health Communications, Inc.
            3201 S.W. 15th Street
            Deerfield Beach, FL 33442–8190

Cover photo ©Jerome Dancette, Fotolia.com
Cover and interior design by Lawna Patterson Oldfield

FOR MICHAEL, ELIZABETH, AND AMY,

AND THOSE WHO SO GENEROUSLY AND COURAGEOUSLY

SHARED THEIR UGLY TRUTH.

CONTENTS

Part Four: OVERCOMING UGLIPHOBIA

INTRODUCTION

*"There are, in every age, new errors to be rectified
and new prejudices to be opposed."*

—SAMUEL JOHNSON

"I am ugly."

The scene is an auditorium at Vanderbilt University in Nashville, where about one hundred people—most are young women with eating disorders—are attending a conference on body image. So far my keynote speech is going as planned. With three little words I can see I have caught people's attention and even made some of them squirm in their chairs.

"No, really," I continue, raising my voice a bit for effect, "I . . . am . . . ugly."

I see a few heads turn as women consult their seatmates. I imagine they are asking each other something like, "Did she really say that?" I press on.

"But don't feel bad for me. Because *you are ugly too.*"

Bold? Perhaps. Rude? Definitely. Insulting? Absolutely. According to the standards and etiquette of public speaking, I had broken three rules: I insulted myself, I insulted my audience, and I allowed an ambiguous silence to take over the room that ultimately led to grumbling and discomfort. I had also used the taboo word *ugly* (I sometimes call it the "U-word") out loud.

Of course I meant to shake up the audience, because I wanted to go right to my topic for the night—the silent struggle that just about every one of us wages every day when it comes to appearance. As a therapist and a woman living in twenty-first-century America, I am well-versed in the issues of appearance and body image. I knew that as soon as I came on stage, some (if not all) of the people in the audience were assessing my clothes, my hair, my face, and my body, and comparing themselves to me. They weren't judging me deliberately. Some weren't even doing it in a conscious way. They were, instead, reflecting one of the most prevalent obsessions in our society—the fear of being ugly—and trying to cope with its effects on a minute-by-minute basis.

In my personal experience, my therapy practice, and my other job as an academic, I have devoted years to studying this phenomenon—the deep and constant fear that we are ugly—and I have recognized that it is the source of enormous and widespread suffering. In my talk at Vanderbilt's "Love Your Body Day" celebration I "came out" on the issue by sharing my own feelings and struggles, and offered publicly, for the first time, my own understanding of this "ugly problem," including its sources, power, and terrible effects.

As the night wore on I would gradually reveal that when I called myself and everyone else "ugly" I was calling attention to our society's ever-changing and impossible standards for appearance and the futility of trying to keep up with it all. The rules, as promoted by the media, cover everything from your scalp to the tips of your toes, and no one, not even a professional beauty (model, actress, etc.) can keep up with it all. This means that by certain definitions we are all ugly at least some of the time. In fact, given the constantly growing list of things we're supposed to do in order to avoid being ugly, failure is inevitable. Under these conditions our self-esteem and well-being may depend on accepting that by some measures we are all ugly, and that it's not the end of the world. To put it succinctly: I'm ugly. You're ugly. And so what?

But before I discuss my philosophical response to the ugliness issue—including my effort to defuse the power of the "U-word"—I'd like to share something of my background, explain the origins of my interest in this issue, and describe the ways that I have explored it. Ugliness is a difficult, emotionally layered subject that can provoke anger, anxiety, self-doubt, and grief, even in people who believe they understand it. We all have these feelings because we have all felt the pain and/or fear of ugliness on one level or another. In sharing mine, I hope to encourage you to keep reading even if you feel sadness, outrage, or hatred for me. Confronting the complex issue of ugliness is uncomfortable, but it is the impulse to turn away from it that makes it impossible for us to affect it in any positive way. And of course, if I'm going to ask you to begin the task of examining your own encounters with ugliness, then it's only fair that I do so too.

Although it came into focus through my work as a therapist and professor, this topic—ugliness and its meaning—has been percolating in my mind since I first realized that "pretty" and "ugly" mattered a lot to the people in my family. They desperately needed me to be pretty. I couldn't have been older than five, and yet I was keenly aware of how women dressed, moved, and posed themselves in the media as well as in real life. I understood, almost innately, that the ones who were considered beautiful possessed a certain power to attract and manipulate others, but that this power depended on their ability to maintain their appearance against the ravages of time and maturity.

According to the legend I heard as a child, my mother had been one of those beautiful women. With blue eyes and high cheek bones, she was tall, thin, long-legged, and athletic. These qualities defined beauty in my family, and my father affirmed its importance by talking about how amazing it was that he, a short, balding guy, nabbed such a stunning mate. The subtext, of course, was that her beauty had been the main thing that got her attention, love, marriage, and, presumably, security.

The story of my mother's allure was told and retold by my parents, but it was always a little confusing to me. By the time I came along, my mother actually lived according to her belief that she was ugly and that this reality made happiness impossible. In fact she had been diagnosed with severe Parkinson's disease at around the time I was born. I never knew her when her movements were not spastic and robotic. I never saw her face except when it was semiparalyzed. The mother I knew was also agoraphobic and profoundly depressed.

As I later figured out, my mother's depression and self-imposed isolation were caused not just by her disease but by her reaction to the idea that she was ugly. My father was affected in a similar way and acted as if my mother had intentionally betrayed him. He also let me know that he valued women primarily as objects of sexual desire and social status. This came out at odd moments, like when we took walks to a comic book store in our neighborhood. The store was near a lingerie shop. My father would stop and stare, and I had to literally push him away from the window filled with bras. His panting excitement was supposed to be funny, but it made me upset to see through his behavior that a woman's appeal—her sexiness and beauty—mattered so much to him.

My father's behavior and my mother's example presented a disturbing reality for a little girl contemplating the future. Beauty was supposedly a woman's most valuable asset—especially where men were concerned—and yet illness, aging, and ugliness were inevitable. Worse was the fact that as I grew up, I had to accept that I was starting out with some disadvantages. I didn't look at all like my mother in her good days.

I was born cross-eyed and needed thick glasses and five surgeries to fix my vision and, more importantly, make me look presentable. I was also put at a disadvantage by our family's lack of money. Though my father had once been well-off, his fortunes were in decline. Before I came along, the family had moved from a mansion to a more modest house. After I was born my father's business failures forced us to move out of our house and into one of the few lower–middle-class apartments available in an otherwise wealthy area. Every morning I would worm my way through a hole in the fence around the apartment complex and pop into a pristine neighborhood of estates where my school was located. Compared to my classmates, I was poor. And it showed. The few clothes I had were dated and shabby. My socks were held up by rubber bands that made grooves in the skin below my knees. My sweaters were pilled and ill-fitting cast-offs that had been worn first by my two brothers.

My brothers, who were four and eight years older than me, were acutely aware of my appearance, especially my weight. This concern was partly a product of the times. I was born in the mid-1950s and came of age as fashion moved decidedly against larger women. By the time I reached adolescence I had received countless warnings about my weight, including admonitions from one brother who worried I'd ruin my chances of snaring a husband or becoming a glamorous secretary or airline stewardess. (At the time flight attendants, who were almost all female, were subjected to severe weight restrictions, which prevented anyone who wasn't thin from winning a job and led to many being fired when they gained a few pounds.)

When I was nine, my eldest brother gave me his high school graduation photo as a keepsake and wrote on the back, "Watch your weight and your complex." The word *complex* referred to what he saw as my negative outlook on life. I suspect I was very discouraged at the time by my prospects. I could see how important it was that I avoid being ugly; I was a poor, overweight, cross-eyed kid. And what about my mother? She had supposedly been beautiful but was rendered wretched by disease. If disease and/or age eventually made everyone ugly, what was the point?

Under these circumstances, the warning for me to watch out for my weight and "complex" was probably a clumsy expression of concern for a young girl who was obviously pained and confused. My other brother, who was even less, shall we say, *constructive*, mocked me mercilessly and encouraged his friends to bark at me because I was "an ugly dog."

The values I was taught and the experiences I endured as a child instilled in me a dread fear of ugliness. Phrases like *ugly as a dog* or, worse, *ugly as sin*, which were aimed almost exclusively at females, stuck in my mind and made me think that there could be nothing worse than to be regarded as an ugly girl or woman. After all, sin represented an offense against God. If your appearance was so grotesque as to be an offense to God, what hope could you have for finding acceptance or happiness within the human family? It was a terrifying prospect.

As an adult I have gradually calmed this fear and found a balance that allows me to recognize myself as a whole person and to feel happy and grateful about that. However, I still face challenges. For example, when one of my daughters was in high school she came home one day to tell me that her boyfriend's father had advised him against marrying her because she was destined "to get fat like her mother." This little incident, caused by a shallow and insensitive remark, made me feel angry, self-conscious, ashamed, and exasperated all at once. It eventually became an opportunity to talk about what really matters in life and the values expressed by anyone who would say such a thing, but I was still upset. And there are times when I'm working with a psychotherapy patient and the subject of appearance makes me lose focus on my work. This happened recently when a patient named Wendy resumed our work together after a two-year break.

Wendy: You look great! Lost weight? Changed your hair? It's darker, right?

Me: Well, I did stop dyeing it.

Wendy: You stopped dyeing your hair? Don't you have ugly gray things coming out of your roots?

Therapists who say they maintain their focus no matter what are lying. This little exchange about whether I had lost weight or changed my hair diverted me for a moment as I thought about my decision to "go gray" and what it meant (more on this later). But then I was able to return the focus to Wendy, who has her own deep concerns about her appearance, especially her hair, which she hates. Imagine how difficult it is to go through every day thinking that something so obvious as your own hair is ugly. This thought would make you so self-conscious, worried, and distracted that it would be impossible to feel relaxed and secure. Sadly this experience is shared, to one degree or another, by every single person I know. It is the crux of what I call "The Ugly Problem."

Indeed, I have come to believe that in developed countries like the United States, the fear of ugliness causes more widespread unhappiness, angst, and agony than any other social phenomenon. At the same time, bigotry based on appearance seems to be the last socially accepted bastion of prejudice. Hateful jokes or observations directed at a religious, ethnic, or racial group are now out of bounds in polite society, but it's still okay to sneer at someone's body, face, or hairstyle.

I know that I am making some big claims and that it is almost impossible to prove them empirically. But in my experience and through extensive research, I have become convinced that the number of people who suffer over the fear that they are ugly, and experience frequent feelings of rejection and loss associated with their appearance, is greater than the number who are harmed in a direct and everyday way by poverty, racism, or other social ills. In fact, I have never met a woman who can claim she isn't tortured, if only just a little, by the ugliness problem. She may resist admitting it or get angry at me for prodding her out of her denial, but invariably she winds up saying, "Yes, I feel it too."

But it's not just the widespread nature of this problem that moves me. I have been profoundly affected by the depths of the despair felt by individuals who have been burdened by the label of "ugly" and the struggle they make to simply go on with life. For example a young woman whom I'll identify by her initials—K.W.—recently explained to me that she grew up hearing that she was ugly, and that her fear that she was in fact hideous makes her shy and withdrawn on good days and suicidal on bad ones.

"White, blond, tall, and skinny is pretty," she said, and since she is African American and Puerto Rican, she'll never meet the standard. When she tried to discuss her feelings with a cousin, he responded with shocking cruelty. "He said, 'You should just kill yourself,'" recalled K.W. 'Without you, the family hotness average would increase, since, let's face it, we're all eights or nines, and you're a five at best.'"

K.W.'s experience is extreme, but it helped me to understand the pain experienced by women and girls across society. Her suicidal feelings are the ultimate expression of the self-doubt we all feel. And her cousin's callous words were really just an honest distillation of the message that our culture—especially the mass media—delivers to us every day.

Perhaps because it is an issue that is "hiding in plain sight" and therefore hard to recognize, little direct research and writing have been focused on ugliness as a social and personal problem. A few intellectuals like Umberto Eco have confronted the issue in a historical or abstract way. Others such as William Ian Miller and Charlotte M. Wright have examined pieces of it by considering literature, biology, and art. But the works of these writers are part of a very small canon, especially when compared with the effort made to examine beauty and its power. The last two decades have seen dozens of writers address looks and appearance, while giving only glancing attention to the concept and cost of ugliness. I suspect this is because ugliness is so painful to consider. It's easy to talk about beauty and the struggle to maintain one's appearance. It's much harder to discuss how we reject others, and ourselves, because of ugliness. My deliberate effort to understand ugliness in all its contexts began with raising questions about the subject in a variety of settings, including dozens of one-on-one interviews. I asked men and women of all ages about their self-image, how they acquired their understanding of ugliness, and how their fear of being unattractive affected them.

The topic of ugliness—how it is defined, what it means, and how we react to it—is never easy to broach. Many people initially deny that it affects them, or are so squeamish about discussing it that they try to change the topic. But once a conversation gets going, most acknowledge that they have, at one time or another, suffered profound loss of self-esteem, anxiety, confusion, and even symptoms of depression because they feared they were ugly. I even collected the words and terms that people associated with ugliness and found that the list was seemingly endless. Among the more common ones were:

mean, self-absorbed, hurtful, ignorant, superficial, sick, nasty, fake, judgmental, condescending, hypocritical, defensive, angry, disappointed, sad, dirty, gross, disgusting, filthy, bad skin, ugly feet, cold-hearted, selfish, fat, unfortunate looking, lazy, sinful, unhealthy, low energy, not caring, poor self-care, old, big feet, crooked teeth, bad hair (kinky, thin, bushy, tangled), unattractive, dry, scaly, calloused, bunions, hammertoe, yellow nails, smelly, cracked heels, fungus, funky toe length, large toenails, bizarrely small toenails, big nose, crooked nose, enlarged pores, acne, dark circles, hairy, jiggly, scars, receding, tired, sick, wrinkled, droopy, grey hair, baby belly, tracheotomy scar, sick, weak, disabled, unconventional, deformed, diseased, disproportionate, unruly brows.

The list above is by no means comprehensive, but the variety of terms suggests that ugliness is a major concern for people. Otherwise, we wouldn't have so many different words for it.

More proof of the broad nature of the ugliness problem came when I expanded my research by posting a statement and a question on the largest online community for women I could find: All Facebook Females Unite in One Group. The statement explained:

I'm writing a book about a topic that has plagued me my whole life . . . feeling ugly and believing I'm ugly. I'd really love your feedback on this topic, because I know I'm not the only one . . . in fact, I don't know anyone, especially any woman, who doesn't believe there's something ugly about her. If you want to write to me privately about this, you can send an email to me: Toni@velveteenprinciples.com. (I've written a couple of other books called *The Velveteen Principles* and *The Velveteen Principles for Women*.) Or you can post here; either would be terrific help with my research . . . and maybe we can support each other in the process.

The question I asked—"When do you feel ugly?"—was purposely simple and direct. It suggested no judgment or criticism, and invited women to speak openly about specific feelings and experiences. I received hundreds of responses from around the world. Many wrote "I feel ugly every morning when I wake up." Variations included "When I first look in the mirror" or "When I start to get dressed for the day," but the point was always the same. Ugliness is a day-to-day concern for just about everyone. And if you open a conversation about it in a safe way, you'll hear unanimous agreement. Almost everyone says that the fear of ugliness affects them in a much more powerful way than the desire to be pretty, and that they would be far happier if they could be free of the pain it causes them.

In time, and with the help of many hundreds of women who replied to my question, I came to realize that we all fear ugliness in large part because we are all ugly in some way, at least according to the definitions offered by our society. And whether we admit this fact to ourselves in a conscious way, deep down we know it's true.

When I spoke at Vanderbilt, I saw many heads nod in assent as I explained that while I am as beautiful as any creature on earth, I also weigh more than average, I am small-breasted, and I have wide hips. But even if I possessed a perfect figure, I might nevertheless be considered ugly because my hair isn't lustrous, some of my pores are enlarged, and I have bunions on my feet. And even if I could erase *those* imperfections, I'd still have to do something about my less-than-toned arms, the surgical scars on my belly, and the cellulite on my thighs.

As I ran through all the "flaws" that make me "ugly," the women in the audience started to laugh. They knew that I could go on for a long time because women are familiar with the whole process of examining the condition and appearance of every inch of their bodies from the tops of their heads to the bottoms of their feet. They laughed even harder when I turned to the rack of clothes that stood on stage, to my right, about ten feet from the lectern.

The collection, which had travelled to Tennessee in my luggage, represented the confusion that had swept over me when I packed for my trip. Starting with an outfit that my twenty-year-old daughter had called "matronly," I revealed the painful process I had followed at home as I tried to decide what I would wear onstage and how I finally threw up my hands, put everything in a bag, and made my husband take it to the airport.

Dozens of women applauded my suitcase confession. I then concluded my wardrobe review by grabbing the last item on the rack, which was a nightshirt made out of soft cotton decorated with a retro-style print of smiling turtles. "This is what I would love to be wearing right now," I said, "But then you would really see my thighs and the shape of my body without camouflage, and I'm not sure you can handle it."

For the next hour we shared memories, insights, and feelings about the issue of ugliness. This exercise was aided by the half a dozen "women's" magazines I had picked up at the airport in New York. As I held them up and read just the headlines and cover copy, we all recognized that these journals present a panorama of worry for the women who read them. Although I was not at all surprised, many were shocked to learn that every single person in the room harbored the secret fear that he or she was irredeemably and objectively ugly. We spent considerable time on the question, "Shouldn't we try to look our best?" and the obvious corollary, "Who decides what 'best' is?"

I know that I *feel* better when I am smarter, more insightful, less petty, more open, and more relaxed, but how does that look? In our society the standards for what is ugly and what is not are set outside ourselves and change practically daily. Trying to keep up with it all is impossible. And when we fail, we feel vulnerable to judgment and rejection.

At one point in the discussion a hand was raised and a thirty-something woman in an elegant flowing black dress stood to protest.

"I think we are all beautiful," she said. "I mean both physically and as people, we are beautiful. Why can't we accept that?"

Of course this protest is valid. Anyone with a halfway open mind would have looked around the room and recognized beautiful features from every corner of the planet and seen real art in the way the women had dressed themselves, applied makeup, and added jewelry and other accessories. They were delightful people, full of energy, intelligence, and grace.

However, it's important to remember that these were also women who had come together because they struggled every day to deal with eating disorders and problems like body dysmorphic disorder (BDD—an obsessive tendency to see oneself as distorted and grotesque) that are related to the ugliness problem. Many of the women in the audience had been hospitalized for their disorders, and everyone in the hall knew at least one person who had died as a result of their fears of ugliness. They may have said "We are all beautiful," but they also knew from personal experience that our dread of ugliness can have fatal effects.

A skeptic who questions the connection between the fear of ugliness and modern problems like anorexia and BDD could argue that people have always feared ugliness and worried about their appearance. History and biology suggest this is true. But it is also true that until recently schools like Vanderbilt saw no need for body image support groups because this fear had not grown into a life-threatening problem. Not so long ago, our ideas about beauty and ugliness were less extreme and our suffering over appearance was less profound. Anorexia wasn't even named until the 1870s, and it wasn't until the 1970s that cosmetic plastic surgery became widely available and socially accepted. Just a few generations ago, no one would have believed that middle-class people would spend billions of dollars a year on diets, hair dyes, and other remedies for the signs of aging that were considered natural and unremarkable.

Taken together, the eating disorders, surgeries, and frantic attempts to stop the effects of time are the symptoms of an epidemic of what might be called "ugliphobia." Like all phobias, ugliphobia is an extreme fear that has a negative effect on one's ability to function and find happiness. In this case, the fear can manifest itself as the rejection of everything that could be ugly, but it may also appear as the fear that you are ugly yourself. I have observed this fear in myself and in many of the people I have treated in more than twenty years of psychotherapy practice. This phenomenon has seemed to worsen as time has passed, growing more widespread and more severe, especially among women.

How big is this epidemic? Is it something new? Answering these questions is difficult. No surveys have been done to assess the extent of ugliphobia, and the modern social sciences are so new—little more than a century old—that historical comparisons present a real challenge. However, repeated studies have shown that a substantial and growing number of us are dissatisfied with our appearance. The unhappiness starts early. One study shows that by age seven, one-quarter of Swedish girls have cut back on eating at some time to make themselves slimmer and therefore prettier. In the United States the figure reaches 81 percent by age ten.

The growing scientific evidence of our unhappiness about our appearance is sobering, but I am more urgently inspired by the suffering of people I know. Over the years I have collected hundreds of comments and observations from men and women who carry with them a burden that is typical and ordinary in a way that should outrage us all. I will quote them at points in this book, so that the focus never strays too far from the human reality. Typical is this observation offered by one of my therapy clients, a woman named Mandy:

> There are absolutely days that I can stand in front of the mirror, and I honestly hate everything about myself and my body. I can pick out about a million places on my body that I hate. My poochy belly, legs, ankles, double chin, droopy breasts, flabby arms, fat short fingers, crow's feet, laugh lines, gray hairs, stray hairs on my face and chin, peach fuzzy sideburns, my cellulite-ridden butt and thighs, stretch marks galore, need I go on? I've always felt ugly.

The self-criticism expressed by Mandy is highly specific—she knows exactly why she hates how she looks—but it also echoes the feelings of every person who measures herself against an unrealistic modern ideal that no one can reach. My main goals in exploring the struggle we wage over ugliness are to discover the source of this pain, describe its many effects, and search for alternative ways of feeling, thinking, and behaving. I also hope that by breaking the taboo that prevents most of us from talking about ugliness, I can encourage others to consider the ways that the attitudes and values we bring to the issue of appearance affect the quality of our lives, relationships, and society. While it may be true that ugliphobia has always been part of the human condition, I believe that because of the pervasiveness of mass media, the consequences of this fear are deeper and more painful than ever.

Fortunately, the same communications technology that is often used to pressure, belittle, and discourage us around the issue of appearance can also support the kind of conversation that leads to empathy, compassion, and ultimately a better life. Let's begin the process here and now.

Part One:

ORIGINS

1

SURVIVAL OF THE LIKED

"It is better to be beautiful than to be good."

—Oscar Wilde

"I'm sorry, but I'm not going to feel bad about trying to look my best. Everyone can be beautiful, and I feel better when I know that I look good. There's nothing wrong with that."

The speaker was a middle-aged African American woman named Danielle, who stood up in the middle of a women's studies seminar to make her point. She wore a lovely silk dress and practically glowed with energy. Defending her desire to be attractive had taken some courage, especially in a room full of people talking about how they resent having to spend so much time and money in an effort to meet impossible beauty standards. Danielle explained that she liked "being beautiful" and felt happier and more confident when "I look good."

Danielle's comments led to a conversation about the positive aspects of fashion, makeup, and accessories. Many of us said that a great pair of earrings can bring real delight. Others swore by the power of a certain shade of lipstick. But there was universal agreement on the subject of shoes. We may have differed when it came to design, color, or texture, but we all knew that the right shoes can have an almost magical effect on our appearance and mood. (We love shoes in part because size doesn't matter nearly as much with footwear as it does with other items of clothing.) This conclusion was reached by a unanimous show of smiles and laughter.

With her protest, Danielle had made a vital observation about human nature—that we all feel a strong desire to be attractive. This feeling is, in part, based on biology. After all, what we perceive as "beautiful" often indicates, in a physical way, that a man or woman is healthy and a good prospect for producing robust offspring. Indeed, people who say that we must choose between caring about how we look and resisting prejudice based on appearance set up a false dichotomy. We don't have to abandon our interest in fashion and beauty to make a statement about being serious and open-minded people. Nor do we have to reject those who take a strong interest in how they look as frivolous or shallow.

At the seminar, the women who supported Danielle offered a spontaneous demonstration of another human trait—our desire to create or participate in safe and accepting communities. Those who listened and then joined Danielle's sentiment with their own comments about shoes, jewelry, and lipstick were showing support for her point of view and for her as an individual. In short, they were making sure she knew that they *liked* her.

We are careful about what we say and how we look because we want to be liked. This imperative, the drive to be included and welcomed—and avoid rejection—means that appearance matters to us whether we are seeking pleasant company so we can pass an hour at a party or hoping to find someone who might find us appealing as a sexual partner and a life-long companion. It is based on the two most elementary and primal biological pursuits of every living thing on earth: survival and reproduction.

Mammals, birds, reptiles, and fish all rely on physical displays—showing their beauty, strength, or vigor—to attract sexual partners. Because animals breed without the benefit of cultural cues, the reproductive advantages enjoyed by the more beautiful bowerbirds or wolf spiders (to cite two well-studied examples) are entirely biological. Humans have a similar inborn preference for pretty. Scientific evidence for this trait has been found in children as young as three months by researchers who showed that they focus more intently on pictures of beautiful faces than on images of ordinary looking people. (The intensity of an infant's gaze is a widely accepted measure of their interest level.) By six months, babies are actually more accepting of women deemed attractive based on the symmetry of their faces.

You don't need studies and experiments to know that first impressions based on physical appearance guide men and women to either approach someone or stay at a distance. Based on our first glance we either feel drawn to someone or we don't. People often refer to "good chemistry" or "bad chemistry" as they describe this force, and it turns out that this slang is more accurate than we know. Although people assume this process is highly subjective and based mainly on individual choice or taste, it is in fact a rather primitive process. The way another person looks actually produces changes in the chemistry of our brains, which sets off a cascade of responses that we can control only in a limited way.

At first glance our brains unconsciously assess a new man or woman for basic signs of health and well-being. In all cultures, males and females alike value smooth, unblemished skin (please stay with me even if you don't have smooth skin—it gets better) and a reasonably symmetrical face and body as markers of good health. When we detect these qualities we feel warm and receptive. Deviations from what is considered attractive or "normal" cause us to feel neutral or even negatively toward the person in front of us. This is why we sometimes feel as though we don't like someone before he even says a word.

Writing in the 1970s, Daniel Berlyne, an influential expert on aesthetics, theorized that it is the uneasiness people feel when confronted with a physical anomaly—discolored skin, a missing limb, a visible tumor—that causes them to conclude that a person is ugly. We feel uneasy, he suggested, because we are wired to home in on differences, like the house cat that enters a room and instantly discovers the new pillow on the sofa or the package on the table.

If we decide that someone *isn't* ugly, because she fits into our basic idea of how a person should look, we then move on to consider qualities that are specific to their gender. In men, broad shoulders, a narrow waist, and defined muscles suggest good genes and therefore good reproductive potential. In women, the cues include mature breasts and a waist-to-hip ratio of about 0.7. These measurements are part of the basic geometry of appearance, which has been observed and described by Aristotle, Plato, Leonardo DaVinci, and, in 2009, the famous plastic surgeon Francis Palmer of Beverly Hills, who developed a 100-point system for rating every face. (He believes beauty is so important that his scale also suggests your potential "for life fulfillment" based on appearance.)

If we like what we see as we assess the people we meet, we'll use our other senses to make further judgments. The sound of a voice—high female voices indicate estrogen, low male voices equal more testosterone—feeds information to our brain and helps us determine how we feel about someone. We also take cues from human scents we cannot detect on a conscious level. (Perfumes are sold to help us appeal to a potential partner's nose.)

Because they are biologically based and point to partners most likely to produce healthy babies, these basic indicators for sexual selection hold for virtually all races and regions of the world. Culture will dictate many variations but from the North Pole to the equator, unblemished skin (no matter the color) and facial symmetry are prized. Even when a culture values larger women, the favored waist-to-hip difference tends to the same ratio. For proof, see the 23,000-year-old "Venus of Willendorf" statue unearthed in Austria. With big hips and sagging breasts, this Venus represented the ideal woman of her time and she had the measurements to prove it. (In their best days, so did both Marilyn Monroe and Twiggy.)

In every era, and with every version of Venus, the beauty seen in women has generally been tied to sexual appeal and reproductive viability. Exceptions can be found. The Mona Lisa, for example, radiates beauty without being "sexy." But she is the exception. For the rest of us, being pretty has always been bound up in being attractive, even alluring, in a way that entices some sexual interest. For much of history this element of beauty was generally a subtext in our relationships, implied but not generally spoken aloud or directly. The beauty of a woman was supposed to attract, even inflame, but this power was considered both profound and a little bit dangerous. It was, ideally, mixed with certain virtues like restraint, kindness, honesty, and empathy.

Today the sexual power of appearance is out in the open. Reduced to a single word—*sexy*—this ability to stir desire is practically synonymous with beauty and even prettiness. The word sexy is used to describe everyone and everything from preadolescent girls to 5,000-pound automobiles. Indeed, anything that prompts any sort of admiration at all can be called sexy, whether it's a sleekly designed phone (in 2005, *PC Magazine* called European 3G models "sexy") or a policy (in 2009, President Obama called energy efficiency "sexy").

This phenomenon of equating all that is attractive with sexual allure and everything else with sexual rejection puts everyone, but most especially women, in a terrible predicament. Like every other girl, I experienced it growing up. I knew I was supposed to make myself beautiful, and thus alluring, but this exercise also made me feel vulnerable and objectified. Of course if I didn't succeed at being beautiful, and thus attractive, then I was an ugly failure doomed to be rejected and lonely. And most of the time I felt like I didn't succeed. I would look at the magazine articles

that declared "What's Sexy Now" and no matter what they described—
from clothes, to hair, to body shape—I didn't have "it." And since I didn't
have "it," I thought, *I must really be ugly.*

Ordinary ugliness doesn't disqualify us completely from the reproductive game, but it does generally limit our sexual options. And the uglier
you are, the more you are constrained. I know that this concept is difficult to contemplate. You might even feel yourself getting angry as you
reflect on the argument I am making. Most of us have been scarred by the
superficial judgments of others and would prefer that the world were a
little less punishing. But like it or not, appearance plays a role in almost
all human encounters and, therefore, in almost all relationships.

As infants, we need others to like us so much that they are willing to
take care of us both physically and emotionally. Indeed, neuroscience
shows that the development of the synapses in a child's brain depends on
his interaction with others. Babies raised in institutions and other settings where they are severely deprived of human contact fail to thrive and
sometimes die. In adulthood, active relationships with other people are
essential to maintaining our mental health. Isolation, whether it's the
result of being rejected as "ugly" or our own choice to "go it alone," can
lead to anguish, mental illness, and even suicide, as prison officials and
others have seen in cases of extended solitary confinement.

Suicidal prisoners in solitary and emotionally deprived infants are
extreme examples, but they help us understand that as *The Social Animal*,
which was the name of a seminal text about social psychology, human
beings can thrive only when they are in contact with other human beings.
We need relationships almost as much as we need food, water, and shelter.
And this need is so important that it contributes to a host of emotions—
many of them complementary—that govern every aspect of how we live.

Among the most powerful are love, loneliness, disgust, and empathy.

Although we might imagine human feelings in poetic or romantic terms, they are also physical or, to be more precise, neurochemical phenomena. They occur in a part of the brain called the anterior cingulate cortex, which is a part of the brain that also makes us aware of physical pain. This is why we experience feelings as physical sensations. If we long for the company of friends and loved ones, we may report an aching emptiness in our chests. True love can make us feel warm and as light-headed and intoxicated as any drink or drug. Disgust, caused by the sight, sound, smell, or texture of something we find offensive, can make us sick to our stomachs.

Not surprisingly, we all try to maximize the moments when we feel good, and do whatever we can to avoid pain. In fact, certain emotions can hurt so much that some people will go to great lengths to avoid them. Addictions involving everything from drugs and alcohol to sex and food are almost always driven in part by an individual's terrible fear of one feeling or another. This fear—of loss, or grief, or some other form of suffering—becomes powerful and debilitating as we use things or activities to numb and distract ourselves.

Many of our most primal fears are linked to our need for relationships and community, and the baseline issue of appearance. If reproduction and survival depend on experiencing feelings of love, friendship, empathy, and inclusion—in short, being liked—then they also depend on avoiding the rejection that may come if we are deemed to be unattractive and, worse yet, ugly to the degree that others find us so revolting or disgusting that they turn away.

Our fear of rejection—and attack—also lies behind the uneasiness we feel when someone stares at us intently. If you've ever provoked a dog to growl by staring in his eyes, you know that other animals have the same aversion. Throughout the animal kingdom, the close inspection that accompanies a stare is considered a threat.

Among human beings, the fear of the "the ugly other" begins, sadly enough, with newborns. We are, it seems, hardwired to respond with fondness to a healthy infant's smooth soft skin, round and relaxed face, wide-set eyes, short limbs, and small nose. This preference has been documented in many different ways. In studies where brain function was measured as adults viewed simple drawings of facial features flashing on a screen, a picture of a conventionally pretty baby's face lights up the adult brain more brightly than the image of a homely baby. Cuteness, it turns out, helps cement the bond between parents and their offspring, and makes it easier for mothers and fathers to endure the sleep deprivation and other stresses of early parenthood.

But what happens when a child is not so cute? According to well-established social science, parents are less likely to respond quickly to the cries of a less attractive baby. This tendency has been documented across income groups and races. Even the mothers of fraternal twins will habitually devote more time to caring for the one deemed more attractive. As they grow, the neglected "ugly" children can lag in both their intellectual and social development. So called ugly kids get less attention from teachers, who unconsciously judge them to be less intelligent than others. They are more likely to run into trouble with authority figures—including the police—and to be sexually promiscuous after they come of age.

In adulthood, appearance actually affects income and status in measurable ways. In the United States, where taller men are considered more attractive, the average male chief executive officer is three inches taller than the average American man, and almost one-third of these top executives are six-foot two or taller, compared with just 4 percent of the overall population. One European study found that women judged to be just a little prettier than average earned more per year than those rated slightly less than average. American economists Jeff Biddle and Daniel

Hamermesh have discovered that less attractive people earn 5 to 10 percent less than their peers. Management analyst John Cawley estimates that in our "thin-is-in" society, an extra sixty-five pounds will cost a woman seven percent of her income. The difference holds true even when you account for certain professions, like acting and modeling, which favor the beautiful and may pay extremely well. Whether you look at arborists or acrobats, the pretty ones earn more.

Income and employment data make it possible to quantify certain effects of ugliness with actual numbers. Measuring relationships is harder, but studies of popularity, dating, and marriage all reveal benefits for beauty and an ugliness penalty. This is true in school, where supposedly handsome boys and pretty girls have more friends. Later in life appearance has a significant effect on our pursuit of romantic partners as good-looking women and men have a better chance of "marrying up" into a higher social class and the ugly risk winding up alone. At every turn, people who fall short of the accepted definition of "good-looking" face extra challenges.

The science that links human development, self-image, economic status, and social standing to appearance leaves no doubt about why "looks" matter so much to us. Just as we are biologically programmed to instantly fear and then flee a tiger in order to save our own lives, we are destined as animals to factor appearance into most, if not all of our vital relationships. Ugliness is such a liability for us, as social beings, that we all understand it to be a dangerous condition. And since perfect beauty is not possible, it's quite reasonable for every one of us to feel terrified that our ugliness might be noticed and used against us. This is why beautiful actresses and models tell interviewers that they are insecure about their appearance or have suffered over their looks. The model and actress

Elizabeth Hurley once told a magazine writer that she won't stand up in her bathing suit when she's poolside because she fears having her body judged to be unattractive. Another actress famous for being beautiful, Kate Beckinsale, describes herself as being "monumentally ugly" as a teen and says, "I still have that mindset." These kinds of statements by beautiful women allow them to appear vulnerable and as if they have something in common with everyone else. They are also, in all likelihood, true expressions of their feelings and experiences.

Indeed, no matter how we look, very few of us reach adulthood without being wounded by someone who rejected us because of our appearance. The epithet "you're ugly" is so powerful that only the most confident and self-assured person would be able to hear it and be unmoved. A child who is called ugly, especially if it's a repeated event, experiences it as genuine emotional abuse, which can leave enduring scars. If she is actively rejected by people who matter—parents, siblings, peers—the loss of connection can make her feel as if she is under threat, as if her very survival is at stake. Even the rare child who escapes direct cruelty and rejection learns to dread being ugly whenever he sees and hears it happen to another child. The pain, shame, and fear that appear whenever someone is called ugly are unmistakable.

Biochemical in origin, and then amplified by our social nature, the desire to be liked and the fear of ugliness—and rejection—arise unbidden in every person's heart. Once you know what to look for, you can see both the yearning and fear at work in almost every person you meet and every group you might observe. At preschools, boys and girls both tend to discriminate against children who look "different" and favor peers who look strong, healthy, and pretty. I have observed that at residential centers for seniors, people often seem to choose dining partners based on appearance. Even at the end of life, beauty has a magnetic power and ugliness is something to be avoided.

Because they are such an elemental part of the human experience, the emotions we attach to ugliness and beauty are not shameful and neither are they entirely under our control. They are, instead, a powerful source of the energy that shapes both an individual's identity and the culture she inhabits. Without the desire to be liked (and even loved) and the dread of being cast out, we wouldn't have much of the art, religion, philosophy, or commerce that define modern life. With these motivations, as we'll see later on, we have created a culture that makes us simultaneously desperate to be attractive and terrified that we are not.

2

BEYOND THE BODY WE'RE GIVEN

*"Becoming the new feminine ideal requires just the
right combination of insecurity, exercise, bulimia and surgery."*

—GARY TRUDEAU

"Toni! It's all over, Toni. Time to wake up."

I force my eyes to open and squint against the bright light. I shiver with the cold.

"Hi there. Can you whistle for me?"

I look at the man who hovers over me and slowly comprehend what he's saying.

"Just sit up a little and try to whistle."

The doctor's commands are muffled by the bandages that are wrapped around my head and the effects of anesthesia and pain killers, but I understand him. I rise a little off the gurney and a nurse tucks a pillow behind my back. I try to pucker my mouth and make a sound, but like a kid who tries to whistle with a mouthful of salty crackers, I can't muster a peep.

"That's a very good sign," the doctor says as he turns to my husband Michael, whose eyes are as big as saucers and filled with worry.

"Try again, Toni."

I pucker and try again. Still no sound. But the doctors and nurses smile and say, "You're doing great." I look again at Michael and feel ashamed that I'm putting him through this, grateful for his support, and humiliated by the fact that I've elected to risk general anesthesia and a surgeon's knife, so that I'll look just a little younger and prettier when my first book is published.

Six years have passed since I decided, with great trepidation, that I would get more attention as an author and my books would reach more readers if I had surgery to make my jawline a little tighter and my eyes a little less puffy. I never hid the fact that I had, as they say, "gone under the knife," but from the moment I first considered it I felt tortured by the decision.

Publishing favors authors who are so handsome or beautiful that their picture can go on the front cover of a book. This is because good-looking authors are more likely to be invited to appear on TV shows and in public forums, and this publicity can sell books. Publishers even have a special name for the quality they want: *mediagenic*. Unattractive people may still get book contracts, and powerful writing can succeed, but for women especially, beauty is considered such a huge advantage that agents, editors, and publicity agents inevitably ask, "What does she look like?"

It's hard to blame people who are in the business of selling to the general public for seeking an advantage. And conventional beauty is always an advantage. This is true whether you are selling an idea, offering a creative product like a book, or running for political office. Technology has changed the marketing game. Where once, an author or politician may have been revered for his artistry or social vision, today acceptance also depends on how they look on television and Google images.

This truth is rarely discussed in an open way, but when it is, people take notice. In the mid-1990s, a British member of Parliament named George Gardiner made headlines when he asked his constituents to support him despite his ugliness. "I'm sorry about my physical appearance," he said, "but I was just born ugly." He spoke after another politician, Robin Cook, said that he himself would never be elected prime minister "because plastic surgery has yet to advance that far." Of course Gardiner and Cook enjoyed the advantage of being male. Appearance is less important for men, which made their confessions a bit easier and, perhaps, endearing. However, Gardiner lost the election, and Cook, who died in 2002, never did become prime minister.

As I considered having surgery to make my face look younger and prettier, I weighed the commercial considerations, which included the hope that my royalties would help support my family, against a host of factors that made plastic surgery the wrong choice for me. First, I thought about the substantial risks of injury and even death that come with any operation done under anesthesia. Second, I had to reflect on the values statement I would make with my decision. For most of my life I have resisted the pressure to conform to unreasonable social pressure and encouraged others, including my daughters, to do the same. Finally, I had to consider what surgery would cost in time and money. I don't have endless supplies of either one.

As anyone who has taken the step knows, once you begin to consider the option of "cosmetic surgery" (a term that makes these procedures sound no more serious than something you might pick up at a department store beauty counter) you are already halfway to the operating suite. Allowing yourself to think about "having some work done," leads you to consider all the potential benefits of "taking years off" your face or body with a single choice. It can also change the way you think about the image you see in the mirror. Suddenly you start noticing new lines and wrinkles that might disappear under a surgeon's hands.

For their part, plastic surgeons talk about the rise in self-esteem, career success, and social status that many people enjoy after their procedures. (Data on the benefits of cosmetic surgery, at least in the short term, supports their claims.) Once your mind is open to the possibility, reasonably persuasive doctors can even convince you that their services aren't any more controversial than a hairdresser's.

I battled with my list of pros and cons and was deadlocked at feeling that a "yes" would betray my values, but a "no" would sabotage all of the time and effort that went into my book. In the end the debate boiled down to this: Could I really live with myself if my book failed because of something so simple as the need for a lift or a tuck? With the question framed this way, I decided to accept the reality of the marketplace and go under the knife.

Years would pass, and I would have to start work on this book about ugliness, before I really understood the personal, social, and even biological pressures that pushed me toward surgery. At the time I didn't fully grasp that I was under the influence of a culture that fears aging and physical differences to a truly phobic degree. Nor did I understand all the ways that my own life experience had propelled me toward the choice I made. What I thought was that "getting something done" was a matter of yielding to an unpleasant reality for the sake of some greater good.

With my decision I purchased, along with my surgeon's services, a degree of risk and worry for myself and the people who love me. (People do die during these procedures.) I also joined a long line of women and men—one that stretches back more than a thousand years—who have made similarly risky choices to endure physical pain and invest significant amounts of time, money, and energy in the pursuit of social acceptance and relief from the fear of ugliness.

Evidence of our dogged pursuit of beauty goes back beyond the beginning of recorded history. Archeologists have discovered mirrors that are more than eight thousand years old. (The elite of the Han Dynasty in ancient China considered beauty so important they buried mirrors with the dead.) Socrates advised his fellow Greeks to study their own faces with mirrors to find character flaws, and in the early Christian churches mirrors were used to symbolize the purity of the Virgin Mary.

Excavations at the earliest-known human settlements have turned up jewelry made of gems and precious metals on the bodies of tribal leaders, slaves, warriors, and even women killed in ritual sacrifices. Prehistoric people also decorated themselves with bird feathers, animal skins, and whale bones. Why did people use these early forms of jewelry, fashion, and makeup? The best theories suggest that they signaled status and sex appeal (makeup can mimic the "glow" produced by hormones during ovulation), conferred some religious benefit like warding off evil spirits, and allowed for self-expression.

The ancients could be very particular about the human form. As set down by an engineer and writer named Vitruvius, who died about 15 BCE, the Roman ideal for the human body called for the torso to measure one-quarter the height of the body while the face should be one-tenth. Individual Romans used ornaments and clothing to both enhance their appeal and to camouflage their flaws. Done well, fashion became a kind of deception, suggesting perfection that wasn't quite real.

Although it could have a dramatic impact, the use of clothing and accessories, which are hung on the body, doesn't have the same visceral effects as some of the other practices human beings use to enhance their appearance. As soon as we learned to dress and adorn ourselves we began applying grease, dyes, stains, and pigments directly on our skins. These substances, which have been found in Egyptian tombs from the year 3,500 BCE, were the basis for some of the first cosmetics ever used. Although some of the earliest coloring agents could cause permanent stains, most had only a temporary effect. Men and women painted themselves to frighten enemies and for ceremonial occasions. Makeup was also used, of course, to make the wearer more attractive.

For women, being "attractive" means presenting oneself as healthy and sexually viable. Makeup can aid this effort by covering blemishes and scars that suggest disease. Dyes and other substances used on the lips can cause swelling and color similar to the swelling that occurs with sexual arousal, and makeup placed in strategic spots can draw attention to, or away from, certain parts of the face or body. The writer Lucian observed these practices among Roman women with a little bit of scorn for their extensive use of "powders, pomades, paints" to cover up their flaws.

Often laced with caustic chemicals like alkali, early cosmetics could sting and burn the flesh. But this kind of suffering for beauty was minor compared with the pain accepted by men and women who used fire or blades on the skin to give themselves permanent decorative scars. Scarification, which has been practiced in Asia, Australia, and Africa for more than a thousand years, is associated with tribal identity and rituals. However, it is almost always done for the added benefit of making the body more appealing and beautiful. As African-art expert Susan Vogel of Columbia University has noted, "Scarification and other forms of body decoration were traditionally considered marks of civilization. They distinguished the civilized, socialized human body from the body in its natural state and from animals." The scars created by cuts and burns also prove a person's courage and ability to tolerate pain. The same purposes are served by tattooing and piercing. Tattoos, like makeup, harken back at least to the Egyptians. Piercing is even more ancient. The world's oldest known mummified body, that of a man frozen in an Austrian glacier 5,000 years ago, has pierced ears.

Piercing and scarification seem mild compared with many of the body modification techniques that were developed more recently. In tenth-century China, for example, the rich began tightly bandaging their daughters' feet to prevent them from growing longer than a few inches. The process was painful, often caused infections, and made walking difficult. However, the results, so-called "lotus feet" (the lotus is a symbol of purity and divinity), were considered beautiful, and the telltale "lotus gait" was a status symbol.

The bound foot was a marker of wealth because only the rich could afford to sacrifice mobility and the ability to perform physical work for the sake of beauty. Like every elite convention, foot binding became desired by all classes, and less wealthy people eventually adopted this crippling practice. (If a woman who had lotus feet had to work, she simply put up with the pain and awkwardness.) By the mid-nineteenth century, roughly 40 percent of Chinese women had bound feet. Fifty years later, however, activists began to campaign against this custom, noting how it limited women's lives. Citing health and safety concerns, officials banned footbinding in 1912, and it has now disappeared. Ironically, it was at this time that Western societies began to develop modern cosmetic surgery, which would allow doctors to alter the body in even more dramatic ways.

The first records of what could be called plastic surgery date from about 600 BCE when the Indian surgeon Sushruta wrote comprehensive accounts of rhinoplasties (nose reconstruction) and skin graft techniques. Plastic surgery in these times was used almost exclusively to repair wounds and birth defects, but good evidence suggests that as early as the first century, wealthy, body-conscious Roman men endured elective breast reduction surgeries. In the second century, Roman men and women both began seeking operations to acquire more beautiful noses.

Modern aesthetic operations came in the 1800s as the invention of ether allowed physicians to operate on unconscious patients. American surgeon John Orlando Roe, a true pioneer in the field of cosmetic plastic surgery, saw his practice in humanitarian terms. He argued that his operations liberated "valuable talent (that had) been . . . buried from human eyes, lost to the world and society by reason of embarrassment . . . caused by the conscious, or in some cases, unconscious influence of some physical infirmity or deformity or unsightly blemish."

In this one sentence Dr. Roe described the host of issues that come into play as anyone considers plastic surgery, not just for the repair of an injury or deformity, but to fix anything that might be considered "unsightly." He said that his desire to help people who retreated from life because of their appearance was altruistic. (This was especially true in cases involving deformities like cleft palate.) But as technology made operations less painful, less dangerous, and less expensive, this "cure" for ugliness, once considered an extreme option, was applied much more broadly. Surgery became "cosmetic," and we got to define, for ourselves, what constitutes an "unsightly blemish" that may be holding us back in life.

Today many of the normal changes that occur as we age—sagging, bagging, and wrinkling—qualify for surgical treatment, and, if you want, you can have an operation on perfectly healthy, young body parts. All that's required to change your breasts, your nose, and even your genitals, are the money and the desire. The practice of cosmetic surgery is so widespread and widely accepted that some surgeons will put implants into the breasts of adolescents who haven't finished developing and perform "lifts" on the faces of young adults who don't show any slack in their eyes or jaws. These procedures can only be described as preventive measures taken by those who are terrified that they may one day be considered ugly. They represent the ultimate, bloody, and painful response to a fear rather than a fact.

Although history tells us *how* the changes in technology allowed us to move beyond the body—from clothing and jewelry to pierced ears and then breast implants for teens—it doesn't explain *why* we have been driven to such extremes. The short answer, if you agree that we have a biological drive to make ourselves appear healthy and sexually alluring, is that our genes make us do it. Some biologists might argue that the reproductive success enjoyed by those who attract mates as they alter their bodies would suggest that it is a behavior that confers an advantage. In this way, the desire for sculpting the self could be partly hereditary, like the tendency to take risks or pursue the arts.

I don't know if science will ever identify genes responsible for the impulse to alter the body. I do know that if such genes are ever found, they will give us only part of the answer we are seeking. The rest of the response—the "why" of scarification, piercing, and plastic surgery—can be explained by an analysis of human culture, which makes us so concerned with beauty and so terrified of being ugly, that we will endure pain and take death-defying risks in our efforts to avoid it.

One definition of culture suggests that it is whatever a society regards as superior in the arts, letters, scholarship, behavior, and manners. According to this definition, the Museum of Modern Art in New York is a center of culture and the people who cultivate the exhibits are "cultured." The word *culture* also refers to the act of growing something. Aquaculture, for example, involves growing plants and animals in water. For anthropologists, a culture is a way of living—everything from sexual mores to the organization of the economy—that is passed from one generation to the next.

When it comes to attitudes about appearance, and especially the matter of ugliness and how one should respond to it, I draw from all the definitions for culture. Our arts help us to define beauty and ugliness. The cultural institutions that govern and transmit our way of living—from the family to schools and even religious authorities—define ugly ideas and behavior and tell us how to respond to them. And together, culture in its various forms magnifies and amplifies a fear of ugliness that begins in our instinctual need to protect ourselves.

3

UGLINESS AND THE PURPOSE OF DISGUST

*"Disgust evaluates (negatively) what it touches, proclaims
the meanness and inferiority of its object."*

—William Ian Miller

Ugly. The word is onomatopoeic, which means that it sounds like the thing it represents. Go ahead, say it. "Ug/lee." Can you feel the way the first syllable catches in your throat? It's the sound of a sick person starting to cough up something nasty or a weary observer expressing revulsion or disgust. At a day care center a staff member might consider the prospect of changing a particularly messy diaper and say, "Ugh!"

The sound of the word *ugly* is no accident. The hallmark of culture, language emerged from the sounds early humans made in response to various stimuli, and it makes sense that many of the words we continue to use seem to be almost visceral in the way they hit the ear. The English world *ugly* is most likely descended from Old Norse "uggligr," which referred to "fearfulness and dread." By the fourteenth century the meaning also encompassed anything that was "evil or morally offensive."

Before exploring how we social animals have linked ugliness and morality, let's step back for a moment and consider the ways that the human response to ugly sights, sounds, aromas, tastes, and sensations has served us over the eons. Like all animals, we use our senses to avoid dangers posed by poisonous or decomposing plants and meat. The feelings of disgust we experience from foul odors keep us from getting too close to germs that could make us sick or kill us. Disgust moves us to either flee or confront ugliness by cleaning it, disposing of it.

Considered this way, disgust evolved in us as a biologically protective instinct that allows us to avoid danger. Similarly, the concept of ugliness, or rather our ability to label certain things as undesirable, hideous, and even disgusting, permits us to place things we want to avoid in easy categories. We don't have to think about the ugliness of a rotting carcass or a rabid beast that is foaming at the mouth. We avoid these things automatically. The same goes for things that feel ugly to the touch or sound ugly to the ear. Retching sounds are disgusting to people the world over, and they make us instantly check for the source so we can avoid contamination.

The fear of contamination, of becoming sick and perhaps ugly if we remain near to things or people who disgust us, is an important component of the human response to ugliness. This feeling generally arrives unbidden, in response to the sight, sound, smell, or touch of something ugly, and we typically react to it without thinking.

But as we reflect on the somewhat depressing facts, it is important to recognize that our concept of ugliness and fear of contamination depend on a mix of nature and nurture. We can have little doubt that putrid smells disgust us on a visceral, even biological basis. The same is probably true for our tendency to avoid people who look sick or severely deformed. The sick provoke our fear of death. The deformed seem to be poor choices for reproduction. In both cases, the human animal is likely to reject what seems ugly on a biological basis. This is the "nature" side of the equation.

However, we also learn what is disgusting or ugly from family, peers, and our community. This is the "nurture" side of things. A good example of this process can be seen in some rules and customs that restrict what people eat. Religious prohibitions on the consumption of pork, for example, can be traced to the ancient realization that some diseases borne by pigs can be transferred to people who eat their meat. Over time people who subscribe to these rules in a wholehearted way can come to regard pork as a disgusting food. They can't abide even the idea of eating it and have trouble understanding how anyone could.

Most of us only realize the full power of our fear of contamination when we find ourselves in a situation where we want to overcome it so we can care for someone who is going through a particularly ugly moment. This happens when we want to help a person who is sick or suffering. These moments, when we can overcome our natural revulsion and fear, occur fairly often in the lives of parents, medical workers, and others who deal with human beings when they are most vulnerable. Ironically, they often come with a feeling of intimacy and warmth, because in overcoming our disgust, we offer acceptance to the person in need.

As it turns out, beauty is not an accurate indicator of long-term health. This was shown by S. Michael Kalick and his coauthors in a study of the long-term health of people who were rated for attractiveness in their youth. As they reported, "relatively attractive" people were "mistakenly rated as healthier than their peers." This kind of information could help change attitudes and bring out the brighter side of human nature.

Serious research has shown that in modern times, our preference for people with certain body types, features, or hair color has absolutely nothing to do with physical health. (Likewise, big breasts in a woman or square shoulders in a man do not predict fertility or healthy offspring.) So, while disgust at the sight of another person may have saved lives in ancient societies, it is now no more useful than that vestigial organ, the human appendix. And, of course, it has caused far more suffering.

The most compelling examples of the dangerous side of disgust revolve around the signs of age and infirmity that inevitably overtake every living person on earth. In some cases and some cultures, the old are respected and even revered. Things get complicated, however, when age is accompanied by sickness or a change in appearance that might remind others of the inevitability of disease, decline, and death. A face full of deep creases and wrinkles will announce that time has taken its toll on your body. Add some discolored teeth, some moles, and a few stray hairs coming out of those moles, and you have someone so ugly she might be called a witch.

I say "she" because witches are generally considered to be female, and the burden of ugliness falls disproportionately on women. Known by a hundred other names—crones, hags, banshees, and so on—witches can be found on every continent and seem to emerge out of every aboriginal religion. In fact, witches appear so early in the various histories of different cultures that they seem to arise almost as soon as people begin to use language and start searching for stories and fables to explain the human condition. Age and decay—sure signs of ugliness—are given human form in the face and body of the witch, who must be feared, avoided, and, if necessary, killed.

Fear and hatred for the witch can spread through a community via a process called emotional contagion. In extreme, acute situations, an emotional response surges through a community like wildfire, and people get caught up in a kind of hysteria, which makes it extremely difficult for people to think clearly and logically and makes mob rule possible. Emotional contagion was behind the panic that accompanied Orson Welles's *The War of the Worlds* broadcast in 1938, and it energized the Salem witch trials of the late seventeenth century, which saw twenty people put to death and more die because of conditions in prison.

The witch trials represented emotional contagion at its most destructive. More typically, feelings are transmitted gradually, in the way that a flu virus might work its way across a city. People "catch" the idea that a certain person, or type of person, is "ugly," and then pass it on through their attitudes, body language, and conversation. Political leaders can spread feelings through their rhetoric and policies. This is how one nation learns to hate another. Similarly, moral leaders like parents, teachers, or clergy pass on attitudes that connect ugliness with other negative traits, like sinfulness and ethical failure.

Like ugliness itself, the witch is generally associated with terrible moral failings that match her horrifying appearance. (In stories, witches typically kill and even devour children in the same way that age devours youth and beauty.) In fact, ugliness and evil are so intertwined in the persona of the witch that in some of history's darkest moments, mobs routinely killed old women on the assumption that their appearance alone proved their sinful nature.

In modern times we don't believe in witches, but we still kill off—in certain ways—women who are deemed old and/or ugly. Old and ugly women (and to a lesser extent men) face discrimination in social settings, employment, education, and even the arts. (Just ask any actress over forty about the roles available to her.) I suspect that on some instinctive level, women who are older are rejected because they are no longer reproductively viable. I also believe that we make others uncomfortable because we are living reminders of the inevitability of decline and death, a reality that is, for many, the ultimate evil.

The ugly-equals-death-equals-evil equation is the natural corollary of the human tendency to believe that everything that is beautiful is good. Tolstoy said, "What a strange illusion it is to suppose that beauty is goodness." I would offer the same assessment of the notion that ugliness equals evil. But Tolstoy and I cannot change what most people believe. Indeed, as humankind has sought to find cause and effect in the universe, to suggest that something other than random chance determines fate, blessings have almost always been attached to beauty, and punishment has accompanied ugliness.

Early societies associated everything positive in life, including bountiful harvests and all the gifts of nature, with beauty, goodness, and beneficent gods. Graphic depictions of goodness were dominated by light and bright colors: the blues, greens, and yellows of a safe and welcoming world. Beautiful heaven is a warm place of sunlight, clouds, and brilliant blue skies. Conversely, misfortune and loss were historically linked to ugliness and angry or evil spiritual beings. Those gods who were truly malevolent were imagined as horrible-looking devils and hideous monsters. For example, Set, the ancient Egyptian god of evil, was described as a man with the head of a jackal or a pig. Chernobog, a Slavic god of evil, was a batlike figure with horns and blackened wings.

Ugly gods could be blamed for every trouble imaginable, from a debilitating deformity to a natural disaster. And given the natural desire to believe that human beings have some power over their own fates, it was logical for the ancients to assume that the poor souls who suffered actually deserved their fate. The ugliness on a man or woman's outside either reflected the condition of the soul or represented a punishment for some evil thought, word, or deed. A birth defect might even be blamed on a mother or father's evil transgressions, or it could be considered a sign of karma, delivered by a just universe, for a misdeed committed in a previous life.

The impulse to regard ugliness as a sign of evil can also be seen in the way that human communities have historically identified the "other," whether it's another tribe, another race, or mysterious interloper, as definitively ugly. As the very first leaders to take a band into combat knew, it's much easier to rally your forces against an enemy who is both ugly and evil, than to fight and kill people who appear physically and morally worthy. No doubt the men of Sumer believed the people of Elam to be hideous and corrupt when the two clans fought the first recorded war in history in modern-day Iraq almost five thousand years ago.

In ancient literature and art—the best sources for early cultural norms—foreign lands are filled with ugly monsters. Whether it was a dragon, a serpent, a Cyclops, or the Cerberus (a vicious three-headed dog), explorers and warriors could expect to confront ugly creatures that were not just disgusting but also horrifying and frightening. The myths about these creatures made the exploits of the brave seem all the more exciting and laudable. They reinforced the cohesion of a community by encouraging individuals to stay close to home and declaring both the goodness of "us" and the wickedness of "them." And they reflected certain innate human fears. No monster served this purpose any better than Medusa.

Part Two:

UGLINESS AND CULTURE

4

MEDUSA

"*I saw you once, Medusa; we were alone.*
I looked you in the cold eye, cold.
I was not punished, was not turned to stone—
How am I to believe the legend I am told?"

—May Sarton

Thousands of years after she was first described as a monster, the mythical Medusa still holds the power to terrify us. Do you recall hearing her story when you were young? One of my brothers actually introduced me to the Medusa myth. Eight years older than me, he went through a period when he was so obsessed with her that he would often draw her picture—complete with the snake hair—and make sure to show each one to me. He was about fifteen. I was about seven, and I found these pictures, as well as Medusa's story, absolutely terrifying. Weren't you chilled by the idea of a hideous snake-haired woman with the power to turn people to stone if they merely *looked at her*? What an awful prospect it would be to confront her. More awful still was the notion of being her.

Medusa's origins are hazy. By one account she was the daughter of Echidna, who was half woman and half snake, and Typhon, who had a hundred dragon heads on each hand and was the largest and most deadly god of all Greek mythology. In this version of the tale she was one of three Gorgon sisters—the others were Sthenno and Euryale—who had sharp fangs for teeth and brass claws for hands. All three hated men, but Medusa was the most dangerous. Her ugliness was so powerful that anyone who gazed upon it was turned to stone. Similarly, she could fix her stare upon anything—a flying bird, a tree, a fish—and petrify it in an instant.

In a second, more widely told version of the Medusa story, which was recorded by the Roman writer Ovid, she was not born ugly. Instead she was a beautiful virgin who entranced every male who saw her. While serving in the temple of Athena, this Medusa was raped by Poseidon. Sexual politics being what they were at the time, Athena blamed Medusa for defiling the temple and punished her by making her so repulsive that anyone who saw her turned to stone.

Medusa's death is the same in every telling of the legend. To fulfill a bold promise, a young hero named Perseus called on several gods to help him pursue and kill the awful monster. Approaching as she slept, he used a reflective shield he had received from Athena to avoid gazing at Medusa directly. He then decapitated her with a special sword he had received from the god Hermes. According to the myth, the winged horse Pegasus and Chrysaor, a giant boar, were born from her bleeding neck. And though she was dead, Medusa's head retained much of its power. Perseus gave it to his sponsor Athena, who placed it on her aegis, which was a cloak-type garment that made her invulnerable to her enemies.

As described in the myth, Medusa remained a powerful and hideous Gorgon—useful for frightening enemies—from antiquity, through the Middle Ages, and into modern times. In all this time she served as the ultimate cultural expression of ugliness, its danger, and its power.

Carved into plaques placed on doorways or drawn onto banners and capes, Medusa's image was most often used as a sign of warning, to ward off enemies and strangers. The archeological museum of Naples houses a 2,100-year-old mosaic that shows Alexander the Great wearing a breastplate decorated with Medusa's fearsome head. In the sixteenth and seventeenth centuries, Cellini, Caravaggio, and Rubens all produced notable Medusas. The painting by Rubens, which showed the severed head staring up from the floor, blood oozing from the neck and snakes slithering around, is especially gruesome. In the nineteenth and twentieth centuries, Medusa was the subject of many celebrated paintings and sculptures, including Salvador Dalí's *Perseus*, which showed the young man holding Medusa's head aloft, by her hair.

But even as artists and writers continued to promote the terrifying and ugly Medusa, some of her attributes defied the idea that she represented only ugliness and evil. The legend held that Medusa's blood, which produced Pegasus and Chrysaor, had fantastic life-giving properties. Wherever drops fell from her head they gave fertile life to the earth. If she was so bad, you have to wonder how her blood could have such powerful life-giving magic.

Then there was the whole matter of the rape, in which she was the victim. Even the most heartless judge might wonder how she was supposed to defend herself from a god. And finally, what about the way that Athena, Alexander, and others deployed Medusa's power of protection? If she was so evil, why was her face used to decorate everything from coins to temples and art created to honor the powerful? Wasn't her real, original power her virginal beauty? Isn't it possible that men hated her, and Athena envied her, because she was so compellingly beautiful? I wonder if Medusa's ability to the turn men to stone isn't an echo of the beautiful maiden's ability to cause erections in men. It's also possible to hear, in the Medusa myth, the idea that the hearts of others were turned to stone, making them unable to respond to her as a human being.

Until the early twentieth century, prevailing academic wisdom held that Medusa had always been categorically evil and that her image was used to frighten enemies. This analysis allowed experts to explain why the ancients deployed such an ugly goddess, but it didn't quite resolve the question of why she was so ubiquitous.

One of the first modern investigations of Medusa was conducted in the early 1900s by a professor of art and archeology at Princeton. In 1911, Arthur L. Frothingham was at the height of his power and influence—he cofounded the *American Journal of Archaeology*—and was hardly a radical. But he nevertheless challenged what he termed the "orthodox" view of Medusa with a paper that concluded that she "was not an evil demon or bogey, but primarily a nature goddess." In taking this position he rose against the giant of his field, William Ridgeway of Cambridge University, who had endorsed the long-standing view of Medusa as a grotesque beast.

For years Frothingham had been able to accept modern interpretations of Medusa only by choosing to ignore evidence that ran against conventional wisdom. He was most troubled by the fact that his colleagues had unearthed thousands of Medusa plaques, friezes, statues, and mosaics, which had been created over a period of more than ten centuries. In countless examples—on cups, walls, vases, and statues—she seems not ugly but beautiful. She also appears to represent not fear, but hope—not death, but life. On coins and on vases she frequently appears with Apollo, the physically ideal god of sun, light, and truth.

Other experts had said that when she was pictured alongside symbols of beauty and fertility Medusa served as a contrasting figure. But the Greeks rarely worked with contrasting figures, noted Frothingham, and he could also point to Medusas in artworks where she joined not one, but many other positive mythological figures. Further investigation of

Medusa in art and literature led him to believe that before she was very bad, Medusa was very good. Indeed, she was, in the beginning, the Great Mother of the world, and there were no snakes in her hair.

Tracing her back to the Minoans on Crete, Frothingham finds Medusa at the center of a civilization that revered female gods more than male ones. Using artwork dated between 1600 and 800 BCE he charts the transformation of the "Mistress of Wild Things"—who tames snakes, lions, and other animals—into a more ugly and frightening character. The change coincided with the rising power of Greek civilization in Crete and the transfer of religious power from females to males. Much of mythology was changed in this time, with males even taking control of birth as Athena emerges from the head of Zeus.

As Frothingham notes, very little in early art was merely decorative. Images were crafted to communicate important ideas and values. He argues, convincingly, that a powerfully positive Medusa was purposely kidnapped and remade as monster. A witchy creature so ugly that the mere sight of her was lethal, she could serve good only in her death. Severed from her body, her head with its open mouth and gaping eyes was a shield and a weapon under the control of another.

When the professor from Princeton rose to defend Medusa and suggest she had been railroaded into a villain's role, he may have stood alone among archeologists, but he was not a completely isolated pioneer. Forty years earlier, Friedrich Nietzsche had already suggested that the evil Medusa had been created to warn against the power of our most basic human passions, most especially sex. She did not exist outside of us, as a threat, but inside of us, as an essential part of human nature. Nietzsche's ideas fed a broader intellectual effort to chart the power of the subconscious mind.

By the time Frothingham put forth his theory of beneficent Medusa as patron of the living world, early psychoanalysts were beginning to explain the universal, but formerly obscure desires and drives that dictate much of human behavior. Under their analysis, common legends, stories, and dreams became an avenue to extensive realms of the mind that lurked just beneath our awareness. These elements of the intellect or personality served our very basic needs including safety, survival, and sexual reproduction.

Sigmund Freud, the most prominent of the psychoanalytic pioneers, made a series of convincing arguments for the power of conscious and subconscious needs and fears, especially those related to sex, that develop and emerge mainly before we reach adulthood. Controversial in his day (his major works appeared between 1895 and 1930), Freud suggested that people harbored deep sexual anxieties that could be discovered and resolved through a long therapeutic relationship. When first offered, his concepts about human sexuality shocked people of the Victorian era. He remains a contentious figure today. However, many of his ideas about our hidden motivations, and the meaning of stories and symbols, have become so widely accepted that they are routinely used to analyze art, history, and politics.

When Freud turned his attention to Medusa, he saw the myth in terms of male sexual fears. Noting that Medusa is always depicted with an open mouth encircled by snake hair, Freud saw first the male's fear of female genitalia. Since men also find women alluring and selective about their partners, he theorized that they need to resolve not only their fear but their frustration and anger. In the Medusa myth we see she is first punished for her beauty when Poseidon rapes her, and disciplined again when Athena turns her into a monster. Still, she's deadly to men. This problem is resolved when Perseus slays her. Freud saw a symbol of castration—the ultimate loss of power—in her decapitation. Pointing finally to the relaxed attitude toward homosexuality in ancient Greece, Freud argued that the creation of a powerful myth about a terrifying woman "was inevitable."

While he dwelled on the way Medusa symbolized what he thought were essential sexual fears, Freud paid scant attention to the more subtle gender politics expressed by the myth. But he did acknowledge that both the "depreciation of women" and "horror of women" were operating behind the Medusa story. Like many of his early ideas, Freud's castration-oriented assessment of Medusa drew only limited support. (I suspect it made even intellectuals uncomfortable.) However, the idea that she was turned into a monster because of a generalized fear of women and the impulse to control this fear has been recognized by many scholars, philosophers, and writers.

Medusa, as these modern writers see her, was first a beautiful goddess responsible for the miracle of life and a stand-in for all women. Like women in general, she held the power of being sexually appealing, and she was at the center of the somewhat mysterious reproductive process that is, after all, the ultimate purpose of all living things. When the Greeks turned her into a monster, and subjected her to a vicious fatal attack, they asserted the power of their male gods to govern the female gods of Crete. In a symbolic way they also expressed a host of feelings and attitudes about women. Among them were:

Women (and their sexuality) are powerful.
Their appeal can make males lose control.
Therefore women are dangerous.
Women must be controlled.
They can be controlled if you declare them ugly and deny them
    power and resources.

As the Greeks responded to Medusa, noting the threat she posed, they denigrated her by making her a hideous monster—not just ugly but murderously evil—and sent a hero to slay her. But the Medusa story is not one-dimensional or simple. Medusa's body and blood, like the blood associated with reproduction, retained their life-giving energy. And even after her death, her head and face remained destructively powerful. This is why Perseus gave her head to Athena. She was the wise patron of Athens and the virginal guardian of sexual modesty, but nonetheless kept Medusa near.

Seen from the perspective of a compassionate woman, the Medusa story reveals first the terrible dilemma posed by beauty and sex appeal. As an innocent maiden who was prized by many men, Medusa was blamed for her own rape, which she supposedly encouraged by being attractive. (The equivalent today is a woman who must answer questions about the way she is dressed after she is attacked.) Punished for being too beautiful, Medusa is rendered ugly and banished. The power in her ugliness is, of course, a reference to the rage anyone would feel over such injustice. But the central message of the Medusa story is that these feelings are also ugly and must be killed before they drive her to do something murderous.

Myths and stories like the tale of Medusa reveal the most essential psychological and social truths. As metaphors, they help us to retain and understand complex ideas and feelings in an instant. As statements about values, they communicate the norms and expectations of our communities. Legends that feature ugly people who are cast out or killed instruct us on the value of beauty and on how our appearance determines our status. The main differences, as we consider these messages from one society to another or one era to another, are matters of style, not substance.

When they rose to power, the Romans appropriated Medusa along with many other elements of Greek religion and culture. Her story was a shorthand warning to all girls, who heard distinct messages in the tale. Don't be ugly or you'll be hated and abandoned. If any part of you might be considered ugly, fight against it at all costs.

5

UGLY AS SIN

"God forbid you're an ugly girl."

—Ani DeFranco

"See-len-see-oh."

Sounded in a deep, basso profundo voice that draws out every syllable and echoes off the vaulted walls, the Italian word *silenzio* sounds like a mournful but insistent command. After a few beats it is followed by the English translation, sung in a different voice but with a similar cadence.

"Sigh-lence!"

The pleading duet comes from the security guards at the Sistine Chapel in Vatican City whenever the murmuring of the tourists gets too loud. The place is a spiritual sanctuary, after all, and their commands, which sound like the mournful bellows of a foghorn, do remind the people in the crowd that they should regard this place with some reverence.

The sad foreboding in the voices of the guards feels appropriate as I sit on one of the benches that line the chapel walls and gaze at Michelangelo's astounding depictions of the essential Christian stories. My eyes move from Adam and Eve's "fall," which shows them transformed from luminous beauty into jaundiced and hunched figures, to the images of Hell at

57

the base of the Last Judgment fresco painted on the wall behind the altar. In this enormous painting, the souls Christ brings near to his place at the center glow with beauty, while those denied his grace fall into darkness. The further a figure is placed from the Lord, the uglier she appears. The lowest of the low appear skeletal, rotting, and deformed. Some have horns on their heads and claws instead of hands and feet.

As I study the faces and bodies of the condemned in Michelangelo's stunning work, the phrase *ugly as sin* enters my mind. It is followed by a flood of cultural associations—imagine a rapid-fire slide show of words and images—that depend on the cultural assumptions that beauty equals goodness and ugliness is evil. Included are:

Stained by sin
Cleansing the soul
Beauty is truth
Truth is beauty
The ugly truth
He looks like an angel
A thing of beauty is a joy to behold
Ugly as the devil
You look like hell
Suffer for beauty
Hide a multitude of sins
Devil's food cake(!)

These one dozen sayings came to mind in less than a minute's time. With just a little reflection anyone could come up with many more. In the ugly-equals-evil category, you could add the sins of gluttony, sloth, indulgence, weakness (moral and physical), and impurity. The beauty-is-virtue list could be expanded to include, among others, patience, self-denial (of food, sex, and other physical desires), cleanliness, and grace in all its forms.

Western society makes these associations—ugly as sin/beauty equals goodness—because for centuries our culture has dwelled on the clash of goodness symbolized by beauty and evil represented by ugliness. Inherited from ancient ancestors, these concepts were adapted by early Christians who argued that pagan gods were ugly, which proved their illegitimacy. Protestants praised "the beauty of holiness" in the Book of Common Prayer and continued to depict sinners as ugly, especially as they suffered in hell. In Pieter Bruegel the Elder's painting *The Fall of the Rebel Angels*, the sinners are grotesque while the virtuous are beautiful. The same is true in the *The Last Judgment* by Rogier van der Weyden, in which a beautiful young Michael the Archangel uses scales to weigh souls. The heavier ones, who no doubt practiced gluttony, sloth, and greed, are sinners consigned to hell, while the lighter souls ascend to heaven.

Early Christians also attached supposed sexual sins—adultery, sex outside of marriage, homosexuality, and others—to ugliness in a way that assumes that unattractive people must be also be "deviant." On the opposite side of the coin, all that was good about people, animals, and even places was associated with beauty. For women, the greatest virtue was often attached not to strong and sturdy figures but to delicate, vulnerable, even ethereal figures who despite their fragile weakness maintain their chastity.

If you consider that historically organized religion was (at least in part) an agent of social control, it's easier to understand the power of the ugly-as-sin paradigm. Believers looked to religious leaders as authorities, and these leaders used their power to establish norms that kept the peace and at least limited the excesses of human nature. Seen this way, it was a good thing that delicate women were sometimes accorded high moral standing. This status probably protected them from exploitation. However, on the other side of the equation, the ugly became vulnerable to socially-sanctioned rejection and abuse. In this way, religion actually amplified and justified whatever biological impulse may lead us to reject people who seem sick, deformed, or even foreign. If ugliness was sinful, we could feel justified in judging, punishing, enslaving, or killing those who seemed repulsive or, perhaps, just a little different from us.

The belief that ugliness was sinful crossed the Atlantic with the explorers who encountered and killed native people, and with the pilgrims who established societies in the new world. In sixteenth- and seventeenth-century America, which was settled mainly by Protestant immigrants from Great Britain and Northern Europe, the concepts of God's blessing and condemnation were part of everyday life. Many of these first Americans believed that health, wealth, and even beauty flowed to those chosen by God, while poverty, illness, and ugliness signaled disfavor. In an echo of the Buddhist concept of karma, you got what your soul deserved. This thinking set the notion of personal responsibility firmly into American culture, alongside the assumption that the blessings of life somehow proved a person to be morally superior.

Fortunately, Western culture has sometimes allowed exceptions to the rules about beauty, ugliness, and virtue. One Christian saint, Margaret of Castello, was a hunchback midget who, according to her legend, was raised behind walls by parents who were ashamed of her appearance. Eventually she became a nun and spent her life serving others. When she died, townspeople demanded that she be buried inside their church. Their priest, who resisted, relented when a crippled girl was healed during Margaret's funeral. She has, ever since, been regarded as the patron of the deformed and disfigured.

Other exceptions to the rule about ugliness and sin are seen in folktales and stories about unattractive characters who turn out to be good souls. The two best known examples of this type of character are the Beast in *Beauty and the Beast*, and Quasimodo in *The Hunchback of Notre Dame*. Both are clearly good and not sinful figures, but sadly, neither is allowed to be fulfilled and happy while ugly. Quasimodo dies without ever realizing love. The Beast is permitted to find and enjoy love, but only after he's transformed by beautiful Belle's tears into a handsome prince. A more modern version of the ugly-but-good story can be seen in Cyrano de Bergerac, but even with his extraordinary wit and bravery, he wins Roxanne's love only in the moment of his death.

As romantic prods inviting us to consider the experience of the ugly person and the possibility that our prejudices are wrong, Cyrano and the other tales taught empathy and compassion. But the difficulty of ugliness was hardly resolved by these stories, and even if you can see the point Cyrano argues against the "ugly-as-sin" paradigm, you won't find much support for this position, even in supposedly advanced and modern societies. Some may say that beauty is only "skin deep" and that you shouldn't judge a book by its cover, but the world we inhabit is filled with proof that the "cover" matters immensely and that our fear of ugliness is far more powerful than our idealistic dream of giving everyone equal consideration.

Culture, as expressed in story, continues to give us one character after another who finds happiness on the basis of her beauty and not much else. From Holly Golightly to Erin Brockovich, it's hard to find a woman in the movies who would be compelling without her exceptional beauty. And of course today, the influence of cultural messages on how we think, feel, and act may be greater than ever.

With the rise of urban communities, technology, and industry, the influence of man-made culture on our sense of what it means to be human has increased dramatically. This culture includes not just the arts, philosophy, and religion but also institutions such as science and medicine, which have sometimes been deployed to support the notion that the outside of a person indicates what resides on the inside. In the nineteenth and twentieth centuries this practice was codified in two bizarre but powerful "medical" disciplines called physiognomy and phrenology. Physicians who used these practices claimed to be able to determine a person's character from the appearance of the face and body (physiognomy) or the shape and contours of the skull (phrenology).

In the twenty-first century, many of us find it difficult to believe that such pseudoscience, which clearly echoed the values of ugly-as-sin religion, was ever taken seriously by intelligent people. But in fact, the idea that physical differences signaled moral deviance was taught at respected colleges and embraced even by intellectual elites who would have claimed to be skeptics when it came to religion. Phrenologists practiced well into the twentieth century and even employed a machine called the "automatic electric phrenometer" to help them identify the supposed misshapen heads of individuals of bad or weak character in a precise and presumably scientific way.

The most disturbing outgrowth of the thinking that produced phrenology and physiognomy came with the rise of eugenics, a social movement that gained real power at the start of the twentieth century. Eugenicists, as they were called, believed they could identify supposedly undesirable men, women, and children by evaluating them physically and mentally. Those deemed unfit, who were far more likely to have darker skin and Mediterranean features, would be discouraged from having children, while those who were judged superior would be encouraged to have large families. Contests were held to find the "fittest families," and eugenic displays were common at state fairs. Invariably these paragons of "positive eugenics" were tall, slim, fair-skinned people of Northern European origins.

By 1920, American eugenicists had focused on improving the national gene pool by preventing ugly and otherwise undesirable young people from ever starting families. Nearly every state in the union adopted a program for identifying these supposedly sub-par children and placing them in institutions where they would be prevented from reproducing. Sadly, tens of thousands of people were surgically sterilized in these places to prevent them from contributing to the nation's gene pool. Thousands more were incarcerated for life.

Eugenics spread from America to Europe where it found receptive ears among the followers of Adolph Hitler. Experts from the United States were given awards by Nazis, who then took their way of thinking to its terrible extreme, beginning first with the institutionalization of the disabled and ending with the Holocaust. (Among the twisted justifications the Nazis used for killing more than six million Jews was that they were ugly and posed a danger to the supposedly more beautiful Aryan race.) The eugenics movement was finally discredited and disappeared after the war when the Nazi horror was revealed. In the postwar period, science showed little appetite for sorting and categorizing human beings, and in many countries, most notably the United States, political movements arose to challenge discrimination based on race, nationality, religion, gender, age, sexual orientation, and disability.

For a time, civil rights campaigns encouraged the hope that all forms of bigotry—even the oppression of people who were called ugly—might be confronted and relegated to the past. With slogans like *Black is beautiful* and forceful arguments for equality, activists made most forms of prejudice shameful. Critics would sneer at what they called "political correctness," saying the social sanction against certain derogatory attitudes and speech went too far. But in general, those who demanded respect for differences had a profoundly positive effect as opportunities increased for women as well as for people of different races, ethnic groups, and nationalities.

On the edges of the civil rights movement, a few voices were raised on behalf of people who experienced discrimination based on their appearance, especially those who weigh more than average. Known as the Fat Acceptance Movement, this informal campaign was kicked off with a rally in New York's Central Park in the summer of 1967. But these efforts were not very successful. Instead, as American society struggled toward dramatic reductions in bigotry overall, inequality based on appearance seemed to increase. The main drivers for this development were the ever more powerful mass media, in all its forms, and the businesses and industries associated with it.

Beginning with print in the nineteenth century and television, which swept the culture in the 1950s and 1960s, visual mass media grew in influence every year as it brought business and industry astounding new tools for selling goods. Present in every household, and in almost every room in every household, television allowed advertisers to promote a vast array of goods using, for the most part, images of beautiful people. A constantly escalating competition for attention required continual improvements in the pitches made to the public. In the race to get attention, advertisers, publishers, and producers turned to more startling images with each new program or campaign.

The end results of the media age have been a beauty ideal more impossible and out of reach than ever before and more discrimination based on looks. (Every month seems to bring a new thing to be worried about and therefore a new reason to fear that we might be seen as ugly.) Confronted with standards for beauty that even supermodels cannot reach without the aid of high technology, just about everyone is left to feel deficient. The fear of ugliness spreads, and so does our desperate desire to avoid it.

The pain and anxiety created by impossible beauty ideals is bad for us but very good for various multibillion-dollar-per-year businesses that have arisen to aid those people—mostly women—who choose to fight the fear of ugly by trying to become beautiful. A significant part of the economy, including businesses that barely existed a few generations ago, depend on this anti-ugly activity for their cash flow. Cosmetics companies, plastic surgeons, media firms, and the vast industries devoted to diet, exercise, and fashion all feed on our real and reasonable fear that we will be treated like a modern Medusa.

6

THE MODERN MEDUSA

*"Just because you are blind and cannot see my
beauty doesn't mean it does not exist."*

—MARGARET CHO

The laughter pouring out of the radio is so hearty and spontaneous that it is infectious. At first you smile, almost automatically, as you imagine tears streaming down the face of the woman who struggles to speak—in between guffaws—as three men encourage her with laughter and approving comments. Then you hear her actual words.

"I like everybody to do well, even somebody that looks like a slapped arse. God bless her. It's like 'You go girl.' She does look like a hairy asshole. She is a lovely lady. God bless her. You just want to say 'god bless' and here's a Gillette razor."

The jokester is a woman named Sharon Osbourne, who is a judge on a television talent contest and the wife of rock star Ozzy Osbourne. Her target, during an appearance on a national radio show, is a Scottish singer named Susan Boyle. In early 2009, Boyle became a worldwide sensation when she almost won a British national talent show. Her stunning voice made listeners take her seriously, but it was her life story and her appearance—middle-aged, overweight, and plainly dressed—that moved viewers' hearts. Here was a woman deemed ugly by conventional standards, and because of it she had faced extraordinary challenges as both a singer and a woman. Then, as if in a fairy tale, she was "discovered" in a talent contest, and her voice won her worldwide acclaim.

In the months that followed Susan Boyle's success, academics, comedians, public commentators, and many others considered how her appearance affected her appeal, and many debated whether she should undergo a "makeover" so that she would look more like other female performers. Those who prescribed plastic surgery, or favored getting her on a diet and dyeing her hair, presumed she would find greater acceptance and sell more recordings of her music if she looked younger and prettier. Others, like writer Letty Cottin Pogrebin, who noted the "years of wasted talent" caused by appearance-based prejudice, hoped she would resist the pressure to conform. More than a few women and men shed tears as they thought about the lives limited—perhaps their own?—by the fear of ugliness.

For a short time Boyle's talent and inspirational story seemed to keep those who would mock her in check. But snide comments and attacks built gradually on the Internet and then on television comedy shows until about seven months later, Sharon Osbourne and her radio hosts felt quite comfortable criticizing her appearance in order to entertain millions of listeners.

"God doesn't give everyone everything," Osbourne said. "I think he gave her the talent."

"Yes, but he really shortchanged her on the rest of it."

"Well yes, he hit her with the fucking 'ugly stick.' "

The male laughter that echoed after the line about the "ugly stick" signaled the audience that Osbourne was a keen and witty observer and the kind of plainspoken gal a man finds appealing. The hosts of the show clearly enjoyed hearing Osbourne put Boyle where she belongs, in the role of an ugly woman who should be ridiculed and rejected despite her enormous talent and warmheartedness.

Ironically, at the time she discussed Boyle in 2009, Osbourne was also known as a somewhat kindhearted person who had suffered in her own way over her appearance. A decade before she had undergone gastric surgery to help her lose a significant amount of weight. She followed this with a series of plastic surgeries including a facelift, breast implants, and multiple skin-tightening operations. Also, Osbourne's own daughter Kelly had been very open about her own experience with critics who picked on her appearance. "I took more hell for being fat than I did for being an absolute raging drug addict," she said. "I will never understand that."

Even with all this direct experience of the pain people feel when they are belittled based on appearance, Sharon Osbourne gleefully attacked Boyle as woman who, like Medusa, had been made horrifyingly ugly by a deity. Crediting God's work with an "ugly stick," Osbourne suggested that Boyle deserved her fate. And what was her fate? To be rejected merely because of her appearance.

As she pushed her into the Medusa role, Sharon Osbourne added Susan Boyle to an endless list of modern women who have been required to serve as cautionary examples of how ugliness is more powerful than any talent, intelligence, or skill a woman might possess. To her credit, Osbourne eventually recognized what she had done and apologized publicly. She said, "I would never want to be responsible for hurting Susan, and I must apologize for getting a cheap laugh at her expense."

I believe that Sharon Osbourne's apology was made, in part, because she knows what it is like to feel vulnerable about her appearance. Unfortunately, very few victims of this kind of attack ever hear words of apology or regret. Less-than-perfect actresses, politicians, singers, and writers—anyone in the public eye—are routinely criticized for their appearance. Powerful women who seek to influence society—Hillary Clinton, Margaret Thatcher, and Oprah Winfrey—are especially vulnerable. By calling them ugly, their opponents can mute their effectiveness with an extremely cheap and ever-ready weapon. According to one insider account, the then-President George W. Bush liked to talk about the size of then-Senator Clinton's rear end. More recently a woman commentator wondered aloud if Mrs. Clinton's mood had been soured because she was having a "bad hair day," and Washington buzzed with negative comments about the appearance of Elena Kagan who was nominated for the Supreme Court.

I suppose that politicians and public officials are always vulnerable to snarky comments, and the derision is just part of the job. But even if your only claim to relevance is as an entertainer, you may still be a target. In most instances, this kind of criticism is done casually, but it may also be planned and deliberate. In 2007, *Maxim*, a magazine for men, offered a formal list of "unsexy" (read "ugly") women that included two star actresses and three pop singers. This declaration was repeated endlessly on the Internet as people around the world agreed that yes, indeed, actresses Sarah Jessica Parker and Sandra Oh and singers Madonna, Britney Spears, and Amy Winehouse were modern Medusas.

Women and men are supposed to laugh at criticism of their appearance, and probably the most futile thing one might say is, "Hey, I'm not ugly." However, the hostility does hurt. Eleanor Roosevelt famously said that the one thing she regretted in her life was that she wasn't prettier. This comment shocks us because it comes from one of the most important women of the mid-twentieth century, and because it betrays the complexity of the Medusa problem. Ugliness is such an awful thing that every woman fears it, including, I suspect, Sharon Osbourne, who as of early 2010 confessed she had spent more than $200,000 on anti-ugly surgeries to lift and tighten her face and various body parts.

When we recognize that Osbourne and the not-so-classically-handsome men who howled about Susan Boyle are themselves afraid of ugliness we can begin to understand what lies behind their mean comments. Like everyone else, Osbourne and company have themselves been subject to the cruelties of a culture—expressed in our families, institutions, and even our art—that threatens all of us with rejection and isolation. To ward off our terror of being symbolically killed off because of our ugliness, we deploy a variety of psychological defenses that are intended to mask our vulnerabilities, shift attention away from ourselves, and soothe our own anxieties. Because the motivations are rooted in the ugliphobia that is almost as common as the air we breathe, much of this is done almost automatically, without conscious intent or choice

From a psychological perspective, Osbourne's "joking" was a classic example of "projection," which involves denying some attribute or feeling in ourselves while ascribing it to others. As she pointed at someone else's ugliness, she projected her own fear of ugliness onto Boyle and diverted any attention that might be focused on her own looks. The power of her words revealed, in fact, the depth of her fears about her own potential ugliness and suggested how much pain she had felt in her own experience with ugliphobia.

As Osbourne tried to pass her shame to Boyle, she played a game of "hot potato," hoping to get rid of the burning emotion that existed in her own heart. This type of projection is a very common, essentially subconscious act that is practiced by almost everyone who has been raised in appearance-related shame and fear. It allows us to be free, if only for a moment, of the unstated and painful worry that we're never pretty enough, that we're the ugly ones.

The men who sat with Obsourne in the studio and amplified the attack on Susan Boyle deployed a slightly different psychological technique: objectification. When we objectify other people we take away their humanity. This allows us to treat them with a level of cruelty we would not normally use against another feeling person. In this case the radio performers denied Susan Boyle any respect for her talent (perhaps because her talent intimidated them) and reminded every woman who might be listening that physical appearance was of the utmost importance. In the process, they revealed their own tendencies to judge women based on reproductive viability, almost as if they were breeding stock.

There is nothing new about the use of objectification to diminish someone in order to excuse abusing them. We can see objectification at work in almost every moment of human cruelty and violence, whether it's the abuse of a child or the horrors of war. Objectification, sometimes communicated with merely a glance, has also been used throughout the ages to disempower women. In a recent experiment Israeli psychologist Tamar Saguy actually documented how women talk less, even when asked to discuss themselves, if they believe a man is checking out their appearance with a critical eye. The difference in the case of the radio program is that technology allows the instant worldwide distribution of the act of objectification. Susan Boyle, who went from obscurity to global fame in an instant, was denigrated in the very same way. And every woman listening heard, loud and clear, that no amount of talent and success can protect you from ugliphobia.

Susan Boyle may have known what she was in for when television beamed images of her face and body, along with the sound of her beautiful voice, around the world. From the moment she began her talent show adventure she was nervous, but as she attracted more notice she grew ever more anxious. When the competition finally ended, and she finished in second place, she checked herself into a psychiatric center for treatment. Sharon Osbourne's mocking comments, which came after Boyle was hospitalized, certainly confirmed that the singer had something to fear—namely public ridicule and humiliation.

Of course, people have been mocked and rejected—and called ugly— for as long as human beings have lived in groups. But for most of human history we have faced this kind of abuse only in the context of our communities. And in our towns or villages, we could also hope to be recognized for something more than our appearance. When worst came to worst, an outcast might even escape to another setting and find a fresh start. But today the rejected experience criticism on a scale one could not have imagined just a few generations ago.

The attention lavished on Boyle was made possible by the global reach of both television and the Internet, which are both relatively new technologies. Fifty years ago, many corners of the world still lay beyond television's reach and the chance of a person being catapulted from obscurity to international notoriety was almost nil. A hundred and fifty years ago the print media could make someone famous, but even the most notable people—princes, princesses, and presidents—could find places where they escaped notice and could move freely. Boyle does not have this option. Wherever she goes, she is noticed instantly.

Fortunately for Boyle, the same technology that provided her critics with a worldwide audience also allowed for her to gain support from those who appreciated her music and were not interested in branding her ugly and therefore unworthy. When she eventually released an album, more than 700,000 copies were purchased in the first week it was available. It was a record for female artists and made her number one on the pop charts. However, her experience as an innocent thrust into the Medusa role compels us to consider how our own supposedly modern culture defines ugliness and then employs it as a weapon in ways that might astonish Perseus himself.

7

YOU HAVE TO BE
CAREFULLY TAUGHT

U-G-L-Y. You ain't got no alibi.
You ugly! Hey! Hey! You ugly.

You're so ugly with a belly full of flab
When you wear a yellow coat people shout cab!
You got eyes like a pig and your nose is big
And with hair like that you should be wearing a wig.

—HIGH SCHOOL CHEER

If you want a definition of ugly, according to the dominant culture, the best source is probably an adolescent female. In every society, they are the ones most attuned to the power of appearance and, consequently, most afraid of being ugly themselves. The "U-G-L-Y" cheer featured above focuses on hair, noses, and bellies, but these concerns barely begin the list of features young women must lament over to avoid being branded as ugly. The standards cover every square centimeter, from the hair on their heads to the soles of their feet, and also apply to how they walk, talk, and even sit in a chair. Indeed, the opportunities for a young woman to be ugly are so myriad that it's impossible to list them all. But I can offer the ones I have heard cited most by my therapy patients who fear they are ugly, because they have:

Dry, oily, pale, dark, blemished, or otherwise imperfect skin
A body that's too fat, skinny, tall, short, curvy, or straight
A big, crooked, bumpy, pug, or otherwise imperfect nose
Short eyelashes, thin eyebrows, thick eyebrows, or unibrow
Brown, blue, green, hazel, or black eyes
Bad breath
Body odor
Red, brown, blond, black, curly, straight, thin, or thick hair
Crooked, stained, missing, too-big, or too-small teeth
Receding gums, gummy smile
Breasts that are too small, too big, sagging, pointy, or asymmetrical
Small feet, big feet, crooked feet, calloused feet, bunions
Nails that are too long, too short, too square, ridged, or dark
Bags and/or dark circles under the eyes
Sunken cheeks or fat "chipmunk" cheeks
Lips that are too thin or lips that are too big
Derrière that is droopy, flat, fat, too big, or too small

If you add requirements for fashion, makeup, and other matters of style, the list of standards for beauty—and *ugly-avoidance*—could go on forever. I like the term ugly-avoidance because it describes the most basic goal that most of us pursue with our so-called beauty regimes. Cosmetic, hair color, and clothing companies may present their wares as elements of beauty, but as often as not, we pluck and dab and dress ourselves with the primary goal of obscuring and covering up anything that others might consider ugly. This is why sometimes we feel anxious, even desperate, as we get ourselves ready for the day or prepare to go out at night. It's not about simply making ourselves beautiful with adornments and decorations. It's about avoiding ugliness at all costs.

Of course ugliness is in the eye of the beholder and an opinion based on cultural standards. Usually when someone calls someone else "ugly," they offer a definition that is not freely chosen, but rather, a parroted version of social standards absorbed over time. (This standard becomes an excuse cited to justify cruelty and prejudice in the same way that ideas about genetics were once used to justify racism and anti-Semitism.) When asked to provide their own, independent definition of ugliness, or for that matter beauty, most of us fall back on the culturally mediated, clichéd concepts. For women living in our time this means ugly is fat, wrinkled, scarred, old, and so on.

Men have their own ugliness inventory, which applies extra penalties to those who are short, bald, skinny, or fat. But the burden on women is far greater when measured in the sheer number of rules for their appearance and the price one pays for failure. In the demanding social marketplace, where appearance affects everything from romance to employment, plain-looking men can overcome their disadvantage more readily than women. Adolescent girls come to understand this truth as they mature and discover the many definitions of feminine beauty and its terrifying opposite. The standards and expectations can be bewildering, and I have heard more than a few people wonder in exasperation, "Where does all of this come from?"

Born first in instinct and emotion, our sense of ugliness is refined and ultimately expressed through culture. Until the modern age, when media and jet airplanes closed the distances between us, the cultural definitions of beauty varied widely from one spot on the Earth to another. Remnants of these differences can be found in isolated corners of the world. Hmong women in Cambodia prefer hairstyles that resemble sheep horns. Some Burmese women still use brass rings to give themselves elongated necks.

Often the specific markers were determined by economic conditions. Where food was scarce, obesity was considered beautiful because it signified wealth. Where food was plentiful, beauty was associated with thinness, because only the rich could confidently forego a meal with the certainty that they could chose to eat whenever they were so moved.

In Renaissance Europe, pale skin became a sign of high status as the rich tried to signal others that they didn't have to work outside, where they might be browned by the sun. In Japan and other societies, delicate women who wore restrictive clothing, like a Geisha's kimono, were obviously high status because they weren't required to move to do physical labor. In these same cultures, a strong, square-shouldered woman in practical clothing was obviously ugly, like a beast of the field.

Modern people living in wealthy industrialized nations signal status—reproductive, economic, social—with variations on the traditional themes. Because calories are cheap and plentiful, being thin indicates that you are intelligently wary of obesity, rich enough to afford high-quality foods, and so strong-willed that you can control your intake. Well-sculpted muscles tell the world that you are not only healthy, but rich enough to invest both time and money in some sort of exercise regime. The right fashions and makeup also announce that you are smart enough to keep up with the trends—as they are communicated in the media—and you have enough cash to continually renew and update your decorative supplies.

In the global village made possible by technology, people in Tokyo, Johannesburg, Rome, and New York all subscribe to the thin-plus-strong-plus-fashionable equation to avoid ugliness, especially if they aspire to be middle or upper class. The heavy influence of the media and beauty businesses based in the United States and Western Europe can be seen in a worldwide preference for fairer skin, straighter hair, and Caucasian features. Hence the rising number of Asian women who get eyelid creases installed by plastic surgeons and the nose job craze underway in parts of the Middle East. In China, some wealthy men and women purchase expensive and painful leg lengthening surgeries to obtain a taller, more Western look.

People instinctively chase beauty and do whatever they can to avoid ugliness so they might be successful in life, or at the very least perceived as successful. Likewise, loving parents want their children to avoid the penalties suffered by unattractive people and reap the benefits that come when you are good-looking. If it were possible to achieve this goal with a vaccine, I suppose many mothers and fathers would line their kids up for shots with as much enthusiasm as they did during the campaign to eliminate polio. But since no one has figured out how to inoculate us against ugliness yet, parents engage instead in a long and unwavering campaign to encourage their children to make themselves as pretty as possible while avoiding anything that might cause ugliness. In my therapy practice it is the rare patient who wasn't regularly warned, throughout childhood, about obesity, posture, wardrobe, and (in the case of girls) the importance of hairstyles and makeup. Even today, I see younger women who are cautioned by parents who worry their daughters won't attract a mate unless they mold themselves to fit conventional stereotypes for beauty.

As the original agents of culture, our families teach us first to identify with the traits and behaviors that they deem beautiful. Sometimes the message is based on a supposedly beautiful mother's example, so her hair, eye color, and fashion sense are held up as the ideal. In other cases, family members will point out examples of beautiful people in every setting, including in the media. (Today's examples, for women, would be thin and toned, with long hair and perfect skin.) Parents, siblings, and others then train us to comply with these standards by giving us rewards—praise, hugs, smiles—when we follow the rules of diet, dress, and cosmetic maintenance, and punishing us with criticism or distance when we fail.

For almost everyone, the more significant motivation is not our desire for the rewards that come with beauty but our dread fear of the consequences we face if we are deemed ugly. Like sex, or hunger and thirst, fear is considered a primary "drive" in all animals, including human beings, because it can motivate us to learn new behaviors that allow us to avoid both physical and emotional pain. As small and vulnerable children we have a primary fear of abandonment, which drives us to do what we can to please our parents. If we feel rejected by them, we will go to great lengths to get back into the safety zone of their approval. As we grow older we seek similar safety in our peer group, and will conform to their rules in order to stay part of the group.

In one of the hallmark experiments in the field of behaviorism, Neal Miller at Yale University showed how even laboratory rats translate pain into fear and quickly master new skills to avoid getting hurt again. To see how this relates to ugliness, consider how an adolescent girl who has been shamed by the "cool kids" will leave the house in a "parent approved" outfit but change into something more provocative when she gets to school. Fear has forced to her to learn new skills, including deception, to avoid pain. Her mother, who may very well ground her daughter for sneaking into a short skirt and makeup, will nevertheless pore over magazines to learn "WHAT'S SEXY NOW!" so that she can stay current and avoid the pain of being ostracized or hearing catty comments at work.

Most of us cope reasonably well with our fears, finding ways to protect ourselves from pain without taking extreme measures. For some, however, an especially bad experience, or a series of hurts, can cause us to focus more intently on what frightens us. The fear can become so intense that we develop a genuine phobia, which drives us to be ever vigilant and fearful. Phobias, which many people associate with the fear of heights or perhaps flying, can have a debilitating, life-altering effect. They can cause people to hide themselves away from others, or abandon their hopes and dreams. But despite what you may have seen in the media, which often depicts people with phobias as crazy or at least a little imbalanced, phobias are not completely irrational. In most cases they begin with real experiences that cause pain that a person hopes to avoid in the future.

Although I think the fear of ugliness causes a phobic response in most of us, our culture is so appearance-obsessed that most of us don't recognize how much time and effort we devote to avoiding ugliness. Indeed as we internalize the values of our culture as taught by families—in this case the definitions of beauty and ugliness—they become essential beliefs. They are so much a part of our identity that we don't even reflect on their origins, and we reflexively pass them on to our own offspring. (For example, I suspect that Kelly Osbourne's anxieties and worries about appearance were in a sense inherited from her mother.) This process means that the widespread fear of ugliness is mainly a sociogenic phenomenon. It may begin in our animal instincts, but it is refined, enlarged, and toxified by a culture that makes sure we all get the message.

No one has been able to track an infant's thoughts, so we cannot know if pretty babies are happier than plain ones. But science does show that good-looking babies and toddlers receive more cuddling, playtime, and conversation from adults. This extra stimulation aids in the development of their bodies and minds. A cycle of positive reinforcement is established, as beautiful children grow more intelligent and confident, and in turn receive more positive regard.

All children learn the importance of appearance as we care for them and eventually teach them how to dress and groom themselves. When we take them shopping they learn the importance of fashion. Later we get them braces for their crooked teeth and, if necessary, surgery for their noses. Most of all, we do whatever we can to get them to *not be fat* because we believe that obesity is one form of ugliness that can be controlled. If our child's weight is not controlled, then others will judge us and him as lazy, stupid, slovenly, and worse.

Experts disagree about the effects of obesity on our health. Significant weight does raise the likelihood of a person's being diagnosed with diabetes. Over time it seems to play a role in cardiovascular health, and it can cause joint problems. But the degree of risk associated with obesity is not well understood, and health concerns are not always the primary motivation behind a parent's efforts to make a son or daughter slim. Often parents are moved by the fear that a fat child will be rejected as ugly by peers, teachers, potential mates, and even employers. It is this fear that lies behind the suggestions, reminders, nagging, and attempts to shame a child who shows signs of gaining weight.

Shame is one of the tools used most often by parents and other family members who think they are saving a child from the pain of obesity. It's employed out of feelings of love—everyone wants the best for a child—that are mixed with fear and, perhaps, a little embarrassment.

"You have the habits of a fat person," said my mother.

"You eat like a truck horse," said my father. Then he'd hold his hands out like he was catching a basketball to show me how wide my legs had become.

I was ten years old, and though I was a little bigger than my classmates, I was not exceptionally large for my age. Nevertheless, my parents were so anxious that I escape the fate of ugliness that they tried to train me to eat in a way that would save me from getting fat. Obesity is a major focus in the battle against ugliness because, unlike height and some other elements of our appearance, it seems like something we ought to be able to do something about. It's also very difficult to hide or get rid of fat once you acquire it. Under these conditions, it's easy to understand why mothers, fathers, aunts, uncles, sisters, and brothers might make a project out of teaching a little girl to eat as little as possible, and using shame to punish her when she fails.

In my case, the lectures, shaming, and deprivation made me feel bad and did nothing to alter my body. Despite years of various diet and exercise efforts I have never been able to be thin, and the struggle eventually left me feeling completely unsure about what and how to eat.

As I have discovered in my psychotherapy practice, this kind of thing happens in many, if not most, families. One of my clients remembers her mother literally taking her dinner plate off the table so she couldn't ask for seconds. Others have told me they were ridiculed as "pigs" or instructed to exercise in order to compensate for big meals. Though poignant, these examples are not unusual. Most of the people I have treated had similar experiences and not just once or twice. In fact, concerns about food and weight are a constant in many households.

You would think that with the average weight for beauty queens and models falling and concern about ugliness consuming more of our time, money, and energy every year, people would be getting slimmer. In fact the opposite is occurring. In 1960, adult obesity rates hovered around 13 percent, and the rate for children was less than 5 percent. Today, almost one-third of adults are considered medically obese, and the figure for children is about 15 percent.

What's going on here? Some analysts have found fault with the quality of food in the modern diet, pointing to higher calorie counts in factory-processed goods. Others note a decline in the amount of exercise we get in the course of our daily lives, thanks to cars, television, home computers, and more sedentary jobs. These factors are no doubt part of the answer, but I would point to deeper psychological issues too.

Beauty has always been considered something rare and difficult to attain. (What would it be worth if just anybody could get it?) In a society where food is abundant and fattening, what could be more difficult than resisting the fats, salts, and sugars that are all around you in order to become exceptionally thin? In this context, the competition to be beautiful involves eating as little as possible and becoming as small as possible.

Although a few people may have exceptional genes that allow them to win this race without suffering very much, the vast majority of us cannot do it no matter how hard we try. Faced with this painful reality, and our dread fear of being ugly, we may turn to food as we become depressed and lose the motivation to exercise. The net effect is that the tiny percentage of women who meet the beauty ideal get thinner and thinner (not to mention hungrier and grouchier).

Later in this book we'll explore the deeper psychological implications of food and diet—including the problem of eating disorders—in greater detail. But before we do, it's important that we understand completely the ways that our social environment makes sure to keep us obsessed with and afraid of ugliness. It turns out that the lessons taught by the family are just the beginning of an education on the fearsome dangers of ugliness that most of us endure for a lifetime.

8

DIFFERENCE AS DEVIANCE

"Deviate an inch, lose a thousand miles."

—Chinese Proverb

In some families children are spared the pain of constant warnings about fat and food and exercise. My client Loretta, who has an African American mother and a white father, recalls that her mother always told her that she was beautiful just the way she was. She even made a point of openly admiring her daughter's "good" hair.

When Loretta was old enough to go to school she discovered she was a member of a minority and that her skin color and features were considered ugly by some of her classmates. As an adult she realized that the rejection she felt at school—because she was "different"—had actually been reinforced by the special attention she received from her mother.

"My mom used to love to brush my hair because I had the best hair in the family. It was thick and straight and stayed where you put it," explained Loretta. In a subtle and unintentional way, this preferential treatment actually made her less secure when she was confronted by prejudice at school. If her mother thought she had "good" hair because it was like a white person's hair, then weren't the kids who made fun of her African features also right?

"I thought that people looked at me and they saw black, and I knew what that meant," she added. "Black equals stupid and criminal and ugly. That's something you have to deal with for your whole life if you are a minority."

Technically speaking, the people Loretta describes as the majority— "whites" of European descent—are a minority on our planet and barely distinct as a group. Genetic research is proving that when it comes to race, most of us are a bit of everything. In fact, we're all likely descended from a band of fewer than a thousand *Homo sapiens* who left the southern tip of Africa about 75,000 years ago and populated the world. And demographers tell us that by 2050, less than half of the people in America will look like the so-called whites of today.

But even when we know the facts about race, we are still affected by the ways in which it is used to define ugliness. Although exceptions abound (including a mixed-race president of the United States), and we can find evidence of a trend toward a more inclusive definition, the images we see in American mass media still favor people who look like they are descended from the passengers and crew on the Mayflower. In order to feel safe and accepted, most of us do whatever we can to comply with these norms. This is why many new immigrants alter their wardrobes and their hairstyles as they seek a place in a new country. They know that the further one deviates from the "standard," the more likely one is to be labeled deviant or ugly.

The word *deviant* is essential to understanding how societies monitor and discipline people for being ugly. In legal terms, "deviance" refers to a deliberate effort to break the law. In medicine it's an illness or condition that marks someone as abnormal. In social settings those who deviate from the norm when it comes to appearance—body shape, clothes, decorations like tattoos—are regarded with skepticism and more likely to be subject to prejudice.

As was discussed earlier, we are a species that prefers to live in groups, and we have a tendency to scan strangers for clues, hoping to determine whether they are safe and worthy of acceptance into our group, or dangerous (ugly) and worthy of rejection. In uncrowded or isolated settings where we might encounter someone face-to-face, we handle this duty ourselves and may even take the time to talk to someone new so we can make a fair assessment. In these one-on-one encounters we might decide that the boy with the Mohawk is a sweetheart or the woman in motorcycle leather is brilliant and creative.

In larger and more complex human settings where one-on-one encounters may be impossible, certain people function as scouts or lookouts who can signal the rest of us when someone new comes into view. For example, the pastor of a small church might inform the members of a congregation about a new member, or the team captain could welcome a new player to a basketball squad. In schools, gossipy students can judge a classmate to be ugly or otherwise inferior and start what several generations of social scientists have called a "reputational cascade" that ripples through the student body. Soon enough, the target is being rejected by students who haven't heard the critiques directly but "know" there's something wrong with a particular kid.

On a large scale, the people who control or contribute to the mass media serve the scouting function. As "experts" they announce whether a new actor, singer, or model gets on the "A-list" or if a new style of sweater or bathing suit is "hot." In media slang the process is called "buzz," and it can be positive or negative. Because human beings naturally feel safer liking what the crowd likes (or rejecting what the crowd rejects), buzz has enormous power to determine what things, people, and even pets are popular. Buzz drives commerce, and it can make or break the career of any person who depends on public approval. As individuals we tend to go along with the trends identified by the experts because they relieve us of responsibility for our choices and can provide "cover" for our negative behaviors or impulses. When women compete over who is most beautiful (and we certainly compete this way), we usually decide the score based on the standards set by these arbiters.

Often the smallest difference can have a profound effect on the popularity of a certain physical trait. This is precisely what has happened with blond hair in the United States. Only 5 percent of American women are born with blond hair, but thanks to the development and marketing of hair dyes, more than a third of us now have blond hair. We have been influenced to change our hair color by Hollywood producers and Madison Avenue art directors who have taught us that blonds not only have more fun, but are richer, happier, and more popular. These claims cannot possibly be true, but as they became accepted, the blond trend passed some sort of tipping point and millions of women accepted it. At some point the trend may reverse, but that would depend on someone with authority declaring that dyed-blond hair is distasteful, even deviant.

Just as parents teach children to value certain traits and fear others, the mass media creates standards and identifies deviance for adults. When *Vogue* and other fashion magazines revive plaids for winter fashion or declare that pastels are "back," we learn what to wear if we want to be accepted by others. Conversely, when *People* magazine runs a photo of a movie star's cellulite, which she will find humiliating, the editors/scouts are telling us to fear the exposure of our own dimpled and puckered thighs. (As we watch this exercise, and perhaps hear the pained reaction of the people who are rejected, we experience a bit of their trauma in a vicarious way. This trauma by proxy reinforces our fears and fosters conformity.)

The scouts are effective because they appear to be authorities or leaders, and they exploit another basic human tendency: groupthink. The term, coined by sociologist William H. Whyte, refers to the way that people in groups prefer to reach consensus, often while following an authority, so they can avoid conflict. You can see groupthink at work in relatively innocuous ways when everyone agrees with a sports broadcaster who criticizes a team manager or goes along when the master of ceremonies invites the audience to applaud a performance. Groupthink can be extraordinarily powerful, especially when you see how it can override both common sense and the truths that people see with their own eyes.

In one classic experiment that demonstrated how people will conform to a group's consensus, psychologist Solomon Asch showed each person in a panel of ten people a pair of cards. One card had a single vertical line drawn on it. The other card had three vertical lines—labeled with the numbers one, two, and three—of different lengths. The middle line—number two—on the second card was obviously identical to the single line on the first card, but when the experimenter asked the participants to match the lines, nine of the ten insisted on picking the wrong one. These "confederates," who were in on the design of the experiment, readily influenced the one subject who wasn't coached to join them in offering the wrong solution to the simple puzzle. The right choice was obvious, but groupthink prevented the subject from making it.

This experiment helps explain why we are susceptible to changing fashions and definitions of beauty, especially when everyone seems to agree on the latest trend. The dynamic becomes more serious when the stakes are high—someone might be harmed—and still the members of the group suspend their own values or skepticism in the interest of getting along with an authority figure.

In the 1960s, psychologist Stanley Milgram demonstrated the power of authority in a study that involved an "experimenter" who ordered a volunteer to administer electrical shocks to a "student" who had agreed to help test the effects of pain on learning. Milgram found that the majority of those ordered to administer the shocks kept doing it even after the "student" (who wasn't actually being harmed) screamed with apparent pain. More than 60 percent actually zapped the learners with a charge that they knew could be lethal. The study, and film showing the subjects in action, became famous around the world as a demonstration of the power of authority.

A few years after Milgram conducted his study at Yale, Philip Zimbardo obtained similar results in the Stanford Prison Study in which young men agreed to play guards or prisoners in a mock jail. The two groups quickly fell into the roles with the guards assuming themselves to be superior and prisoners becoming obedient. Despite the obvious fact that they were all subjects in an experiment, some of the guards quickly became abusive and many prisoners accepted being abused without ending their participation. Although the test was planned for two weeks, Zimbardo ended it after six days when his girlfriend told him she was appalled by his behavior, the actions of his subjects, and conditions in the pretend jail.

Zimbardo's experiment confirmed the power of leaders and the tendency toward obedience and conformity discovered by Milgram. The behavior of the guards in the "prison" also highlighted the way that we treat people whom we consider to be deviant. As supposed criminals, the inmates were stripped of everything that would identify them as individuals, including their clothes and their names. They were addressed solely by their identification numbers.

With the authority—Professor Zimbardo—identifying who was disgusting, evil, and deviant, the guards felt justified in "just following orders" to be cruel. The behavior of the guards worsened as time passed, and they formed a more cohesive group of their own. As a small society, the guards group reinforced the sense that there were standards that the prisoners could violate and encouraged the use of more extreme tactics to control them. Some in the group also acted as monitors of dissent to make sure the people in control maintained their solidarity. These "mindguard" types have a strong need for the safety that comes with affiliating with those in power and become uncomfortable when anyone tries to upset the balance of their group.

Like Milgram's work, the Stanford study also drew criticism from professionals and laypeople who said that Zimbardo had violated the ethics of his profession by encouraging the suffering of some of his subjects. (In Milgram's study some of the volunteers who "shocked" students agonized over their actions.)

Though perhaps flawed, the two experiments became landmarks in psychology because they helped answer important questions about how and why people comply with extreme social norms and orders from authorities. Their results were recently replicated by a French documentarian who filmed ordinary people, who thought they were participating in a new game show, administering shocks to a contestant who answered questions incorrectly. Pressured by the host and the audience, more than 80 percent of the participants followed the rules to deliver shocks that they were told were potentially deadly. The experience and subsequent film were highly disturbing to all of the people involved, as were the Milgram and Zimbardo studies.

Years after his participation in Milgram's study, one of the subjects wrote him to say, "Though I believed that I was hurting someone, I was totally unaware of why I was doing so. Few people ever realize the difference between when they are acting according to their own beliefs and when they are meekly submitting to authority." Milgram's correspondent also said the experience had helped him to become more committed to his own conscience and that this had allowed him to register as a conscientious objector when he was drafted to fight in Vietnam.

Seen from even greater distance, it becomes clear that the Asch, Milgram, and Zimbardo experiments replicated, in a compressed time, the dynamics of authority and groupthink that play a critical role in our socialization. Asch showed that once the standard is set, people will adopt it and go along with it, even if it's illogical. When the stakes are raised, as they were in Milgram's work, people may struggle with unethical commands, but the majority still obey. And when authorities set parameters but then leave decision-making up to the rest of us, we still have a tendency to impose strict control on those we consider deviant. All of these findings affirm the power of culture, socialization, and our widespread fear that we will be judged and punished.

Since human beings have a desperate need for safety, approval, and belonging (which yields access to group resources), the worst kind of punishment is ostracism. This shunning can be subtle or extreme. I'll never forget the elaborate story I heard from a fourteen-year-old psychotherapy client whose clique at school had decided to make a point of ostracizing a group they considered to be their rivals. They even named the opposing group FUGS & Co. (for Fucking Uglies and Company).

The most impressive element of the dynamic my client described was not the pain inflicted on the targets of the taunts and criticisms, but the solidarity experienced by the girls who banded together in hatred. Following their own social leader, they defined themselves as beautiful and worthy, and found safety in expressing cruelty toward others.

This consensus didn't mean that they were objectively correct about prettiness and ugliness. Those determinations are always subjective. But it did give them a measure of social safety and perceived power within the walls of their school. They acquired this power and safety by showing how they could hurt others and that they were willing to do it. Who, after seeing how these girls hurt a classmate, would risk calling any of them ugly? Wouldn't it be safer to join them by agreeing with their definitions of beauty and trying to comply?

It is one of the great paradoxes of human nature that when most of us pursue "beauty," we believe we are practicing a kind of self-expression, but in fact our identity is really found through connection with a group that determines what is appropriate style.

If you are a businesswoman in Manhattan who chooses a particular hair color and invests time and money in getting the best dye job, you may feel you are exercising autonomy by making a personal decision. However, you also know, deep inside, that you are responding to certain social cues. Someone outside yourself has identified the "best" color and declared one salon or another "superior." In the end you didn't choose freely, and the part of you that knows this truth feels conflicted. You may even feel ashamed and angry about going against your higher values.

If we want to understand our own relationship to social standards like "beauty" and "ugliness," Zimbardo, Milgram, and Asch provide a vital conceptual foundation. They explain, in disturbing ways, the effects of social standards on the individual. Whether we like it or not, we are all affected by groupthink and the power of authorities. Our fear of being identified as deviant and being rejected can lead us to abandon our higher values, and the struggle to maintain our identities can leave us feeling wounded and traumatized. When experts tell us who is acceptable and who is not, it is all too easy to become desensitized to others and even to our own humanity.

Part Three:

THE UGLY
EFFECTS

9

CODEPENDENCE AND UGLIPHOBIA

"I'm codependent. Is that ok with you?"

—SEEN ON T-SHIRT

In the famous studies that identified the power of groupthink and authority figures, Asch, Milgram, and Zimbardo created experimental societies that took on familiar characteristics. The participants looked to others, most especially the leaders, for cues and assumed the roles they thought they should play in order to fit into the group and stay safe. Some, most especially Zimbardo's "guards," identified strongly with being in charge. They accepted that the "prisoners" were lesser beings—surely they were considered deviant and ugly—and that as guards, they were supposed to boss them around. Remarkably, the prisoners also fell into line, becoming depressed, less assertive, and self-negating.

Psychologically, the subjects in the experiments all became codependent, meaning that they looked to others to tell them whether they were acting properly or were worthy or unworthy people. Codependence has become a well-known term in the last few decades, especially as concepts related to the addictions recovery movement have become better known. As most people know, addicts and those around them often fall into patterns of behavior that are mutually reinforcing. Without making a conscious choice to do so, a wife, husband, or partner will conspire to keep an addiction secret, because he or she is afraid to face it. If children come along they automatically adjust their behavior in order to get along and stay safe. (This means, for example, that they learn to ignore certain problems, to tiptoe around the addict, and to avoid confrontations.) The hallmarks of families affected by addiction include:

Denial of reality, as the addict refuses to recognize his problem

The numbing or absence of feelings

Chaotic/unpredictable behavior

Blaming and shaming by parents who believe that others are
    "the problem"

Lying to cover up addiction

Insecurity

Highly conditional love

Addicts and their codependents are typically shocked when they discover the elaborate fiction they have constructed to convince themselves they are not suffering. Generally this breakthrough doesn't happen until someone has "hit bottom" and the pain caused by some sort of crisis—a lost job, illness, auto accident, and so on—demands attention. Through therapy, and/or a recovery program, they recognize the power of addiction and codependence and begin to learn new ways of treating themselves and others.

Remarkably, the people who experience a crisis and go through the painful process of discovering the truth are the lucky ones. They get to learn that their assumptions about life are misguided, their feelings can be respected, and they don't have to be crippled by shame. A good example of this is the father who finally connects his violent mood swings to alcohol, accepts responsibility, and begins to change. If friends and family (codependents) follow an addict into recovery they discover that their own behavior, thinking, and perception of reality have been shaped in radical and negative ways by their relationship with someone who is governed by addiction.

Why bring up the dynamics of codependence in a book about ugliness?

The answer is that when it comes to matters of appearance and the standards for beauty and ugliness, we're all subject to the harsh and fickle moods of a society that acts very much like a substance abuser. With the mass media serving as its voice, society bombards us with manipulative messages. We are stuck in the position of the codependent family members, constantly scrambling for security but never quite finding it.

Through the media and the many institutions that transmit cultural messages and communicate values—family, school, businesses, and so on—modern industrialized society delivers a constantly changing set of demands. In one season we're supposed to pluck our eyebrows into a high arch. In the next season we're supposed to let them grow in. The same erratic pattern holds for the fashions we wear, the haircuts that are "in style," and even our choice of makeup. The only thing we can be certain about is that the definition of beautiful will become more extreme with every passing day. First shapely women like Rita Hayworth and Jayne Mansfield were our models, and then we were given Audrey Hepburn, who had almost no curves at all. Gradually the ideal woman, according to the social norm, became a bizarre combination of the two: both willowy and buxom.

Besides giving us an ideal image to live up to, the mass media offers us products to buy and stories to mimic in the pursuit of beauty and happiness. The advertisement for an expensive watch that asks, "What are you made of?" is telling us that we can communicate our real value by purchasing and wearing an expensive timepiece. All sorts of luxury brands offer us the opportunity to claim some status through a purchase, and most of us know, on some level, that this is going on. I know one woman who cannot stop buying designer clothes and has named her dogs, ironically enough, Gucci and Fendi.

Along with advertisements published to sell us an identity, the media advises us on how to "Go from So-So to Sexy!" and how to "Get Gorgeous!" It helps us to be beautiful by selling us laser hair removal kits, zit zappers, and many other "solutions" for problems we need to camouflage, cover, and *conceal*. Whenever I see these words in an advertisement—especially the word conceal—I feel like I'm being urged to deceive others by hiding my real self, as if I am something shameful.

Since we are highly visual creatures—a picture communicates a thousand words—images of beautiful women are essential in getting these messages across. In most cases we don't have to read the words on a page or listen to the voices in a commercial to experience the emotion the advertiser wants us to feel. This is why many of us get a sinking feeling when we merely flip through the pages of a magazine. Each picture of an impossibly perfect-looking woman is yet another reminder of how much we must buy, do, and consume in order to avoid being ugly. It's an endless task and depressing to contemplate because it makes us feel like failures who should be ashamed of ourselves.

Even when the media seeks to inspire us with heartwarming stories, it also offers an appearance-based subtext. Would most love stories succeed if the woman was not beautiful? I think not. On-screen romance stories depend on the female lead being beautiful or just temporarily ugly. The transformation of so-called "ugly ducklings" is a hugely popular theme. In every one of these stories we learn that the fulcrum of a woman's value is her appearance. But take heart. With the right investment in fashion, and perhaps lessons in poise and etiquette, you can become a swan worthy of love.

Remarkable as it may seem, all the love stories, how-to articles, and advertisements for products are supposed to be positive aids that will help us avoid being ugly. They are offered by writers, producers, directors, and editors who typically believe they are supplying important inspiration, information, and advice. The darker side of the media is represented by sources that threaten us with shame if we fail to comply with conventional standards of beauty. As discussed, mythology, religion, film, and television abound with stories that tell us there's almost nothing worse than being ugly—especially for a girl or woman—and that ugly people deserve what they get.

When the media uses shame to attack people for their appearance, it mimics an addict's behavior in a most uncanny way. Shame is the hallmark of addiction because on some level people who are controlled by their use of drugs, alcohol, or some other compulsion know they are out of control and that they are hurting themselves and others. As incidents and outbursts pile up, the embarrassment becomes unbearable and the addict tries to deflect it onto others. Thus, a father who is high and trips over his son's shoes humiliates him by calling him "a slob" in front of his friends. A mother who is too drunk to go to the grocery store criticizes her daughter for "being a pig" when she drinks the last of the milk in the refrigerator.

Because all children identify with their parents, these attacks have real power to shape their self-concept. Of course everything a parent does will influence a son or daughter because children observe, copy, and internalize their parent's style of living and their values. And we don't need to say anything at all to communicate with our kids. An icy silence, raised eyebrow, or stiffened spine can be enough to signal rejection. (One therapy patient told me his mother had a way of looking at him that registered disgust, as if, he said, "She was smelling rotten meat.") The feelings produced in children by these signals live on in the mind long after we're grown (therapists call this the "parental introject"), and they continue to control us. As adults we may not even know where our thoughts and feelings about ourselves come from; we just believe them to be "true."

Sharon Osbourne's extended attempt to shame the Scottish singer Susan Boyle was a telling example of how the mass media can involve us all in a dynamic that replicates life in a family dominated by an addict. Osbourne performed the role of the addict who was so filled with self-loathing that she felt compelled to heap shame upon someone else, just to ease her own burden and deflect attention. As members of the radio audience, we were like the children standing by as a brother or sister is singled out for unfair punishment by an addict parent. We see the abuse, but we are usually too afraid to intervene in the moment, and we fear being targeted ourselves.

Because they produce fear, the shaming techniques deployed by the likes of Sharon Osbourne or, for that matter, advertisers who make us feel insecure about how we look, dress, act, or even smell can control our behavior, especially in the short term. Fear keeps us silent and keeps us buying products. But the pressure of shame, and the bullying quality of it, inevitably creates anger. We naturally resent how we conform to out-side influences, but since we're still frightened by the prospect of being rejected we often turn the anger inward. We think, *I must be the problem* and then redouble our efforts to conform—buying more stuff and adopting more beauty regimes—while we keep secret all of our failures and flaws which are, after all, real parts of ourselves. This is how a cycle of fear, conformity, resentment, and self-denial is established and inter-nalized. We quietly and unconsciously begin to deny our true feelings. Instead of protesting against the social standards by declaring that they are unfair, if not arbitrary, we start to play along. Soon enough we adopt the rules about what is ugly and what is beautiful, and we conduct ourselves as if they really matter.

This occurs not because we don't possess free will but because we often don't recognize that we have the option of making a choice different from the mainstream. The question of free will has long been the focus of philosophers, theologians, and scientists. Some religions consider everything about our lives to be "predestined" by a deity who controls everything. Others hold that God gives us the ability to make choices and that in doing so, we demonstrate our moral fiber. Mark Hallett, a researcher with the National Institute of Neurological Disorders and Stroke, has looked at the human brain and determined that "Free will does exist, but it's a perception, not a power or a driving force." According to Hallett, people "have the sense they are free" but usually don't realize that their choices are limited by context.

The problem of free will is not just an academic concern divorced from the challenges of daily life. Courts have long recognized that people who sign a contract or hand over control of some aspect of their lives must be of sound mind and grant "informed consent." And lawyers who work with plastic surgeons and the surgeons themselves worry about whether patients can and do make their choices freely based on informed consent, a matter that can become vitally import if the outcome is bad and a patient files a lawsuit.

As the African social scientist and writer M. D. Ruel put it, an individual's ideas about beauty are formed in "connection with a reference group" that influences your concept of how a person should look. The reference group may include people you see in everyday life and/or models, actors, and others in the media. (This may explain why women in California who get surgery to enlarge their breasts routinely choose much larger implants than women who have the same surgery in New York. The women they see every day have, on average, bigger breasts than the ones who live in New York.)

Once you consider the influence of the reference group, the writer adds, "The personal decision to alter one's body through cosmetic surgery, although superficially resting within the domain of autonomy, unquestionably implicates the social and cultural forces affecting that decision." In other words, if I get the surgery, I *may think* I chose it to express myself as an autonomous and independent person, but in fact I didn't choose it freely at all.

I believe that most people who have plastic surgery actually sense that they have been subject to outside influence, and so they feel some shame and resignation about how they made such an important decision—one that came with life-threatening risks—without true autonomy. I know this has been my experience, and so I am ambivalent when it comes to talking about it. I suspect this confusion is shared by every person, from actresses who grace the cover of magazines, to our coworkers and neighbors who suddenly look tighter, slimmer, or curvier, and don't want to tell us how it is that their appearance has changed.

Of course, we have lots of other reasons to hide the truth about plastic surgery. For one, we are all supposed to be so naturally beautiful, or disciplined about diet and exercise, that we don't need it. But I think that the shame we feel about making a less-than-independent choice under the powerful influence of the culture is a major factor in our tendency to keep it secret. This shame, perhaps even fear that we'll be deemed weak and insecure, is often experienced subconsciously, but it is what silences us.

I feel great empathy for every person who struggles to adapt to our appearance-obsessed culture and winds up making choices for themselves that never feel quite right. In my own case, I came to regret taking the risk associated with plastic surgery and wouldn't do it again. I recognized this regret when I was diagnosed with a spinal cord injury that required emergency surgery to save me from being paralyzed. As I signed the forms for that operation I thought about how life comes with so many risks we cannot control, and I felt foolish for having taken a serious one in the pursuit of a small improvement in my appearance (more about this later).

I feel less empathy when it comes to mean or destructive behavior. I know that we are all influenced to join the anti-ugly crusade, and that you can find temporary comfort and even approval when you play the game and belittle someone else. Children have been doing this forever, making one member of a group the outcast while the others laugh together. However, adults know that the same culture that bombards us with impossible standards for beauty and frightening messages about what will happen to us if we're ugly also offers us spiritual, philosophical, and psychological tools that help us exercise independent choices.

The golden rule, which tells us to "do unto others as we would have others do unto us," is one of the great gifts of human culture, and nearly every religious tradition in the world offers a variation on this message. Equality and respect for others is taught by many social organizations, from the scouts to the court system. No one can reach adulthood without being exposed to these ideas in one form or another. The trouble is, of course, that many of us have been trained to ignore them and to seek instead the short-term advantage that may come with putting someone else down or choosing to go along rather than risk being hurt ourselves.

As anyone who has experience with addiction knows, adapting to the addict's unreasonable behavior can yield short-term benefits. Children who do this can stay out of trouble. Adults adapt to an addict's strange demands and behaviors in order to maintain the bond of a relationship and whatever benefits—emotional, physical, financial, and so on—they may derive from keeping the cycle going.

Those of us who conform to the cultural definitions for beauty and ugliness may find that we succeed in the competition for sexual partners, a circle of friends, and a job. If we are lucky enough to be born (or make ourselves) truly good-looking, we may even be rewarded with fortune and fame. Corporations that sell the stuff that makes us beautiful (or that prevents ugliness) also gain from our rush to be "on trend," which can cost many thousands of dollars per season. Many billion-dollar industries have been built on making people unhappy with their appearance and desperate to purchase anything that promises to keep ugliness at bay. Every inch of the human body is now subject to cosmetic intervention, which explains why you can now buy products to change the color of your nipples.

However, just as most people who are raised to be codependent with addicts eventually find themselves forced to deal with their dysfunctional ways, almost every person who plays the beauty versus ugliness game must eventually confront her own imperfections. Age, illness, accidents, and swiftly-changing fashion trends affect everyone. Just as the disabled argue that fitness is only "temporary," I would say that "beautiful" in the common sense of the word is only temporary too. If it weren't, then supermarket tabloids wouldn't be able to publish photos of movies stars with droopy breasts, flabby fannies, and bald heads.

We enjoy looking at these photos because they subvert the lies and denial that allow our abusive culture to perpetuate its ridiculous system of rules about appearance. The cellulite on a former Miss America's thighs and the ill-fitting toupee atop a leading man's head tell us that no one can live up to the ideal. They also give us a little *schadenfreude,* which is a German word for the guilty pleasure we sometimes experience over another's misfortune.

Of course, the great irony in this process is that, depending on the moment and the circumstances, we all wind up acting out every one of the roles that occur in the dance of codependence. Sometimes we are victims who hear our classmates laugh at our "ugly" clothes or our pimples. Sometimes we are the abusive enforcers of the rules who, like Sharon

Osbourne, point at someone's supposed flaws and pass that hot potato of shame.

Most of the time, however, we just struggle to find security and connection in a world that can seem threatening and judgmental. Given the limits of genetics, time, and our wallets, we do the best we can with our appearance, hoping that we won't be ostracized. But to varying degrees, we are nevertheless affected by the bigotry and prejudice that swirls around us. No matter what we look like, some part of us suspects that prejudice based on appearance governs many of our relationships and influences our status and our efforts to be happy and successful. These suspicions are reasonable and practically universal.

10

BIGOTRY BECOMES AN INSIDE JOB

"What luck for rulers that men do not think."

—Adolf Hitler

The idea that human beings turn the hatred expressed by others into self-loathing is so well established that the terms *self-hating Jew* or *homophobic gay* are part of the vernacular. We know that these expressions are shorthand for a complex psychosocial process that leads the victims of prejudice to internalize the standards of a perpetrator so that the cruelty directed at them from the outside becomes an essential part of their self-image.

Studies of internalized prejudice have identified the power of social norms and propaganda to promote self-hatred in many contexts. For centuries, depictions of African Americans in plays, song, visuals arts, and media reinforced prejudice and taught the oppressed that beauty was a matter of white skin and straight hair. Whites who controlled society offered rewards—less demanding work, higher social status, education—to African Americans with lighter skin and less curly hair. Under these influences African American society evolved a hierarchy that echoed the prejudice held by the dominant culture, with those who looked most like whites occupying the highest rung.

The persistence of these stereotypes is remarkable. Ask anyone in the African American community about "good hair" and "bad hair," and they will tell you that according to prevailing wisdom the good stuff is straight and "manageable" like a white person's. Black women spend billions of dollars a year on products and services that promise good hair, and in my experience many preschool girls can tell you that hair that is "nappy" or "like a pot scrubber" is a sign of low status. (For a wonderful explication of this issue see comedian Chris Rock's 2009 documentary *Good Hair*.) Much of the emotion and effort that goes into good hair flows, at least in part, from the prejudice of the dominant culture. White America regarded people of African descent as ugly for so long that even the targets of this bigotry adopted some of its cruel judgment.

In prewar Europe, the Jewish community was affected in a similar way by the Nazi propaganda machine, which overwhelmed the German public with depictions of Jews as evil and ugly and made it dangerous to show any outward signs of Jewish identity. Some Jews responded by making every effort they could to deny their identities, and a few even cooperated with the Nazis. More commonly, the bigotry and propaganda produced an internal conflict that made people doubt their self-worth. Historians and social psychologists have studied this phenomenon of self-doubt and how it may have prevented many Jews from recognizing the extreme nature of the Nazi movement. It is easy to imagine that thousands of Jews died because confusion about identity and socially transmitted messages about ugliness clouded their judgment about the hate building all round them. By the time they realized what was happening it was too late to escape.

The self-doubt (and in the worst cases, self-hatred) bred by ugliphobia may also be difficult to recognize because it is practically universal and most of us begin feeling it before we can really attach words to our emotions. In families and then school, children sense that advantages flow to the more attractive girls and boys, and they are correct. Of course, most kids don't enjoy this favoritism. They know they are getting second-class treatment, and because children tend to believe they are responsible for whatever happens to them, they wind up feeling bad about themselves.

Children also learn by watching and listening and sensing that people who are considered ugly are likely to be rejected or abused. No one has to spell out this truth in a direct way. Instead they acquire the inclination to hate ugliness in others and themselves in a casual way, like they might catch a virus. When a teacher shows impatience with an overweight girl who is then taunted in the playground, the unstated message has a more powerful impact on the mind of a growing child than any phrase scrawled on the blackboard.

Daniel Goleman, author of *Emotional Intelligence*, writes that when this happens our "brains interlock" and emotions spread out "like a virus." Holocaust survivor Elie Wiesel uses the metaphor of "a cancer that is passed from one person to another, one people to another." These descriptions are apt because they suggest the power of prejudices to invade our very being, even when they violate our basic sense of empathy and our innate desire for fairness.

Life isn't any fairer in the other great source of life lessons for children: the world of television. According to the Kaiser Family Foundation, American kids spend more time with television than any other source of information. As soon as a child is aware of TV, he can see that on most of the shows aimed at kids (including cartoons) the good guys, heroes, and heroines are usually tall, lean, and fair while the bad guys are short, dark, and misshapen. As he grows and his viewing tastes change, the imagery will not. From the child stars in Disney movies to the men and women who frolic on the beach to sell soda pop, almost every likeable person or character children see on TV will be conventionally attractive. Their beauty will be associated with love, happiness, achievement, and joy, which they express with great big smiles, laughter, and flashing bright eyes. Those who are not beautiful will likely suffer defeat, loss, loneliness, or rejection, and show their sadness with slumped shoulders, downcast faces, and tears of anguish.

Even when they are seen on a screen, from the safety and security of the family home, the emotions in these presentations affect the viewer almost as powerfully as real-life experience. This is especially true for children, whose developing brains are more receptive. Registered in the emotional center of the brain, the amygdala, the images and sounds can raise the heart rate and cause a change in breathing. The experience can teach us any number of emotional lessons, including the idea that we should be quite afraid of ugliness and worried we might ourselves be ugly.

As a relatively primitive part of the brain, the amygdala works with emotions and doesn't generally distinguish between information gathered from sources like the media and real life. Our brains also burden us with "source amnesia," which makes it difficult for us to recall how we may have learned certain facts or acquired various assumptions. Long after we've forgotten whether our parents modeled fear of ugliness or we saw a so-called "ugly duckling" story at the movies, the power of these messages to alarm us and frighten us remains. The emotional content, especially when children suffer what I call "trauma by proxy" from watching hatred expressed on screen, becomes far more important than the context. As time passes they are left only with the feelings associated with the event. They come to "know" that ugliness is bad, even if they cannot explain how they know it. From this point it's a very short journey to hating the ugly and hating the ugliness in oneself.

If I ever had any doubt about the effects of all these messages on the young, they were dispelled when a woman I see for therapy told me about the reassuring words her four-year-old daughter offered when the car wouldn't start at the end of a shopping trip. "Don't worry mommy, you're beautiful and you're married," she said, as if these facts made everything all right. This four-year-old's perspective requires, of course, that she consider what might happen if her mother was not so pretty. At some point it will also occur to this child that she should hope to grow into a beautiful woman and dread the possibility of ugliness.

As children reach adolescence, the influences of media and the social environment become even more profound. Today's more extreme beauty standards, especially for young girls, raise the possibility that by age ten, eleven, or twelve they will be regularly scrutinized and criticized based on weight, breast size, complexion, and other features. Boys come in for their share of judgment, and will start to worry if they are not staying in stride with their peers, but girls get far more attention for their appearance and face frequent and intense comments, comparisons, and stressful encounters related to how they look.

Adolescence is also the time when we first hear "ugly" paired with other very unpleasant and negative words including *stupid, dirty, lazy,* and most especially, *slutty.* By adding these moral assumptions to the evaluation of a person's appearance, we amplify the shame they are supposed to feel. The addition of "slut," which is supposed to describe someone as sexually indiscriminate if not overtly aggressive, affirms that ugliness so limits a female's options for finding a partner that she must "put out" in order to interest someone.

The issues of appearance and sex in the young in our culture are, of course, intensely complex, full of paradoxes, and difficult to unravel. For example, assumed "slutiness" is not just a problem for the ugly. In our culture young women who mature early and those who are extra curvy are also subject to snickering, innuendo, and assumptions based on their appearance. And in a society that is obsessed with the beauty of youth, all adolescents learn, at an ever earlier age, that they are the sum or their body parts, which have value depending on their size, shape, and condition. This reality is taught in fairly subtle ways by advertising and other mainstream media that feature hypersexualized characters, dialogue, and images.

There's no product in the world that cannot be sold with images of a young woman in a bikini, and there's hardly a director around who can resist positioning the camera so that it captures her, at least once, at waist level from behind. This practice of using sexy images of women to decorate ads has been on the increase for decades, as many studies have shown. Sexy clothes—miniskirts, fishnet stockings, spiked high heels— are even put on dolls that are then marketed to prepubescent girls. This use of sex to sell products for children is just the latest twist in a long and evolving practice.

The first widely noted use of a sexualized underage model deployed to pitch fashions for adults was the famous 1980 Calvin Klein jeans ad that featured a fourteen-year-old Brooke Shields. Although the ads prompted much criticism, they did the job of selling clothes, and since then many companies have followed suit, finding gold in the use of models who look underage even if they aren't. Everyone, it seems, places a value on the bodies (if not the minds) of young girls. And lately they are being joined by boys.

In recent years, the lean and hairless bodies of young men also have been used more frequently to the same purposes of selling and titillating. Some of the energy for this trend comes from older women who find a certain kind of justice (turnabout is fair play) in making young males sex objects. While the idea of May-December romances involving older women is not new, it is now being recognized more openly and promoted as something positive, as mature women (called cougars) pursue younger men. The objectification of males has been aided by the proliferation of media, which allows for "niche" marketing to special groups and increased competition among the manufacturers of images, who desperately want our attention.

Recent years have also seen far more attention being focused on ideals of what might be called "male beauty" including height, sculpted muscles, square chins, and stylish hair. Magazines for men now devote far more space to body issues than they did in generations past. A recent "Lose Your Gut Issue" of *Men's Health* included articles such as, "The Easy Way to Hard Abs!" "Your Best Body Ever!" and "Get Back in Shape: See Results in 7 Days!"

Young men, who are under increasing pressure to avoid being ugly, are most susceptible to the pressure to adopt these new standards and match the appearance of male fashion models, actors, and pop stars. I suspect that many of them feel uncomfortable with their objectification. I know that I feel uncomfortable every time I pass by the Abercrombie & Fitch clothing store at my local mall because the managers often post a live shirtless teenage male model at the entrance to the store to greet customers as they enter. It saddens me to see a boy being exploited in this way, and to know that males are being pushed to satisfy a new unrealistic ideal. However, there seems to be no stopping the trend. In an apparent parallel to the youth-is-everything standard for women, the body of the ideal man is supposed to be hairless like a young boy's, even as it's blessed with muscles to match a Greek god's.

One measure of the power of these images is the $19 billion per year Americans spend on health clubs. Revenues at these gyms, used by men and women at roughly the same rate, actually rose higher as the U.S. economy slipped into recession in 2008. Between 2000 and 2005 (the latest available data), sales of men's skin care products rose by about 400 percent and topped $16 billion worldwide. This growth was led by new products, especially electric razors and trimmers, made to help with the removal of body hair, a practice called "manscaping," which became a requirement for males who want to avoid being ugly.

Where did the idea of such aggressive hair removal for men originate? According to Askmen.com, it developed first among male pornography stars who realized that shaving their pubic hair—as their female counterparts do—would make their genitals look bigger. Porn, it seems, now sets the standards for what is beautiful and appealing and what is ugly and undesirable.

As the ultimate media destination for a culture obsessed with appearance and sex, pornography is a $16 billion annual business that grew rapidly in the Internet age. (As of early 2010, five of the top 100 websites in the world offered free porn.) It is so widely available and readily accessed that 90 percent of young people between the ages of eight and sixteen have been exposed to pornographic images. Some social critics see a real crisis in these numbers and argue that adults have failed to protect children from media that is immediately traumatizing.

I have no doubt that some children are upset by seeing graphic images at an early age. But the broader and more pernicious problem is the way that porn, and the rest of the media, sexualize the young and distort their thinking about their bodies, relationships, and basic value as human beings. A recently convened task force of the American Psychological Association reported that our culture's sexualization of girls (meaning the promotion of adult-style "sexy" dressing, makeup, and behavior) has had a decidedly negative effect on their physical and mental health, cognitive development, and sexual attitudes and behaviors.

In media, we are told that if you are sexy and desired, you are powerful and more likely to achieve happiness. Corporations that sell clothing, beauty products, and grooming aids amplify the message by creating style trends influenced by porn. Thongs, super high heels, and corset tops once sold only by Frederick's of Hollywood are now available in every suburban mall. In the drive for ever-rising sales, companies push the limits of marketing by advertising these wares to ever-younger consumers. (Surely you've seen the underwear and outerwear for girls with suggestive words like *juicy* printed on the seat.) This is how we wind up with makeup parties and skin-baring fashions for seven year olds and school-age kids obsessed with making themselves look like models, actresses, and pop stars dressed up to excite a crowd.

What very young imitators don't fully realize is that the perfection we see on the screen and in print is never as effortless as it looks. Except for the occasional behind-the-scenes report, we rarely see the team of stylists, designers, and others deployed to create images of the beautiful and worthy. Young people who wake up every day and try to replicate this look for themselves inevitably feel frustrated as they fail and blame themselves for the fact that the image in the mirror doesn't measure up. Today, by the time a girl reaches high school, she's far more likely than her predecessors to have converted her supposed "failure" into anxiety, insecurity, and even self-hatred.

As we struggle to deal with shame and fear about ugliness, most of us wind up projecting at least some of our pain onto others, hoping to feel better by externalizing the discomfort. Adolescents and young adults can be quite clumsy and crude as they pass the "hot potato" of shame to others. After examining a target—in the same way that we examine models of perfection in the media—flaws are catalogued and then the victim is subjected to mocking laughter, organized shunning, and rumor mongering. The attacks can temporarily divert all the fear of ugliness onto another, but in the long run it instills more worry in all who participate or witness it, as they quite logically wonder, *Could I be the next target?*

Living with fear or the negative judgments of others can be both emotionally and physically debilitating. It raises the level of stress hormones in our bodies, which inhibits brain development and contributes to diseases such as hypertension. One research project done at the medical school of the University of California, San Francisco, actually found that negative social judgments, like being rejected because of our appearance, elevate cortisol levels for a substantially longer period of time than other forms of stress. High cortisol levels can contribute to heart disease, bone loss, insomnia, loss of libido, and many other problems.

Along with our physical reactions, we also experience a psychological response to this fear that may lead us to redouble our self-hatred and then renew our commitment to all the anti-ugly tactics—dieting, exercise, spending—that might protect a person from the victim's fate. Although they originate with standards set by the culture, through repetition, trauma, and continual reinforcement, the feelings that motivate these responses become seated in our minds and we are unable to let them go. We don't think, *I better get on a diet so I can be healthier and happier.* Instead we *feel* afraid of being fat ("ugly") and become determined to address the fear by dieting.

In an interview in late 2009, the twenty-six-year-old actress Gabourey Sidibe, who became famous as the star of the film *Precious: Based on the Novel* Push *by Sapphire*, described how she had internalized the fear of ugliness and spent much of her lifetime trying to overcome it. Considered a cultural breakthrough, *Precious* explored the tragic experiences of an obese young African American woman who is abused by others and struggles to find a sense of self-worth despite being the object of scorn based on her appearance. Even though Gabby had achieved great success as an actor and spoke eloquently about the art and humanity in the film, the headlines in the press about her comments focused on her confession that "my first diet started when I was six years old," instead of what she had to say about her craft or her experiences.

During a widely viewed interview with TV talk show host Oprah Winfrey, the star discussed her lifelong effort to deal with her size, the reactions she got from others, and the way she internalized the rejection she had experienced while growing up. Like so many in her circumstance, she had engaged in a long battle with her own body that involved a great deal of self-hatred. She had lots to say about making films and performing for an audience that would reach into the millions; however, little of this material reached the wider public. Instead the focus was on weight and how, as Gabby said, "One day I had to sit down with myself and decide that I loved myself no matter what my body looked like and what other people thought about my body."

By focusing on Gabby's appearance over her performance, editors and producers who excerpted the interview played to the prejudice that dominates our culture. Many of the reader comments, posted on the website where I saw a clip from the show, reeked of bigotry. "She makes Oprah look thin," noted the very first post on a website I viewed. "Hopefully she can get her weight under control and Oprah as well. I think Gayle [the host's friend Gayle King] is packing on the pounds too. They are all on the buffet tour."

The fact that the website operators who presented the edited interview succeeded in provoking such negative comments, as well as sincere rebuttals from other readers, proved that they knew that everyone is concerned about appearance and worried about weight. By now, we all know that to be overweight is to be ugly, but that dieting, especially when one begins at an early age, can train our bodies to conserve calories and "yo-yo" between a low weight established by a highly restricted diet and ever-higher weights achieved once we stop exercising such harsh control.

This is the terrible conundrum that arises around weight and appearance that is represented by Gabourey Sidibe. We yearn to avoid ugliness by being thin, but the main tool we can employ to lose weight can set us up to be fatter in the long term. It's a vicious cycle that leads us to be at war with our own bodies and to suffer rejection and self-hatred, even if we are talented and successful in every other arena of life. This is exactly what happened with Sidibe, by the way. She has said she began her first diet at age six and like many people she gained back the weight she lost, and more. In "yo-yo" fashion she lost and then gained more every time she restricted her diet. As she got bigger she endured more cruelty from others.

The effects of this struggle against appearance-based prejudice are the same as the symptoms seen in people who have been victims of domestic abuse. They include:

Depression
Alienation
Hostility
Decreased life satisfaction
Declining self-worth
Feelings of trauma, loss, helplessness
Paranoia
Frustration, resentment
Fear
Shame
Compulsive behaviors
Substance abuse

These symptoms arise because like an abuser, the larger culture plays on our human need for connection, makes us vulnerable to criticism, and then exploits that vulnerability with the never-ending threat of rejection. In a way, we are all hostages to this process because it takes place all around us. And like victims who eventually come to identify with our captors—the famous "Stockholm syndrome"—we come to accept the judgment of others. We think, *If only my skin was smoother or my hair was less dull, then I'd be happy.* And if we do manage to improve our complexions or get shiny hair, but feel no relief from the fear and pressure, we'll agree with our captors again by finding something else to feel bad about and "improve."

The ultimate psychological destinations for people caught in this cycle include social anxiety, which can make us dread being with others, and paranoia. I have treated many people with appearance-related social anxiety, and they suffer with such a high level of self-consciousness that it disrupts their lives. Whether they are at work, with friends, or with family, they are constantly checking themselves to make sure that their makeup is right, their zippers are closed, or that their teeth and noses are clean. Worse still are the rare cases when excessive worry and vigilance about appearance lead to paranoia. Although it's impossible to say that worry about ugliness causes paranoia—this is a complicated illness—I have seen it expressed as a truly dreaded fear of being judged ugly. Sufferers believe everyone's looking at their roots, their thighs, and so forth, and this belief forces them to withdraw from contact with others. This was how one woman explained it to me via Facebook:

> I fear if I ever get involved with a guy, he will constantly be looking at pret-tier girls and thinking about them. I am attending university and I feel invis-ible . . . I feel like I haven't made any friends because I'm not pretty enough. I have never felt so alone and neglected in my entire life. I feel as though I'm floating by. I am on academic probation because last year I missed so much class because of the problems I have with my appearance and leaving the house. I can't stop thinking of getting my nose busted into shape and the god-forsaken tumorous curse removed from under my eyes. When I stand in cer-tain lighting and catch a glimpse of my reflection, I am horrified at how bad my bags look; it literally looks like my eyes are melting.

Based on this note it would be impossible to determine whether the writer is truly paranoid, but I have seen her picture and can say that what I see is quite attractive by conventional standards. However, the way she talks about herself is cruel, and her fear of being judged limits what she does with her life. Her fear of going out is a common coping strategy for those who become morbidly afraid that they are being assessed and ana-lyzed. But even withdrawal doesn't provide real rest because when preju-dice is internalized, it is always with us.

11

THE WEIGHT PROBLEM

"You don't know what it means to a woman not to be beautiful . . .
Living only to be loved, and attractiveness being the
sole condition for love, the existence of an ugly woman becomes
the most terrible, the most harrowing of all torments."

—*FOSCA*, IGINIO UGO TARCHETTI, 1863

When sociologist Sharlene Hesse-Biber of Boston College tried to find out what an American woman was "supposed" to weigh, she ran into a surprising level of confusion. The targets set by weight-loss centers and others who made money by defining beauty and ugliness were substantially lower—sometimes as much as twenty-five pounds—than the standards suggested by medical experts. In her own survey of college students conducted in the 1990s, Hesse-Biber found that almost every woman she interviewed believed she should meet the lower, commercially influenced ideal and hoped to lose weight even though every one of them was, according to the best science available, within a healthy range.

"A woman of average height and build will find it difficult, if not impossible, to meet these stringent and increasingly elusive standards set by the cultural trendsetters," wrote Hesse-Biber. Nevertheless, she adds,

"Our culture sets up rewards and punishments to ensure women's life-long involvement in becoming a certain body."

Indeed, a body that is exceedingly slim (with the exception of large breasts) is a more important signifier of beauty and status than a beautiful face, thick lustrous hair, or any other feature a woman might possess. Conversely, fat is regarded as the one true indicator of ugliness, understood by every man, woman, and child in the land. To be fat is so terrifying, and the phobic response to it is so universal, that for most of the recent decade one TV network counted *The Biggest Loser*, a weight-loss competition, among its most popular programs with ten million viewers.

People tune in to watch *The Biggest Loser* in order to see one of their worst nightmares in the flesh—extreme obesity—and to find hope that even the extremely overweight can overcome their ugliness and be beautiful. The huge audience for this program is perhaps the best single piece of evidence for the widespread incidence of the fear of ugliness in our culture today. It is expressed not only in TV shows but in our personal attitudes and behaviors, which have been observed and confirmed with remarkable consistency over time.

Repeated studies begun in the 1980s have found that by the time they reach their teen years, more than half of American girls have been on a weight-loss diet. It's tempting, considering the long-term nature of this behavior, to say that girls and young women have *always* been worried about weight and dieted to be slim, so the research shows nothing but basic human nature. Unfortunately, the results over time show we should be very worried.

Between the years 2000 and 2006, the percentage of girls who told the Harris Survey they believe they must be thin to be popular increased from 48 percent to 60 percent. In the same period the age at which girls begin to express concern about their weight was dropping. In 2010 a Girl Scouts of the USA poll found that 42 percent of girls in the first, second, and third grades said they wanted to be thinner, and two out of every five nine-year-olds said they dieted regularly. According to the Rudd Center for Food Policy and Obesity at Yale University, nearly half of American men and women would give up a year of their life if it meant they wouldn't become obese. Adolescent girls report they are more afraid of obesity than cancer.

What are we getting from all this emphasis on weight? In America obesity rates have climbed for thirty years, and now, for the first time, some states report that nearly a third of all adults are clinically obese. (Twenty years ago no state in the country had an obesity rate higher than twenty percent.) These statistics come with higher rates of diabetes and other weight-related illnesses that pose real hazards to our health. They also point to the chronic confusion, unhappiness, and fear of ugliness—ugliphobia—that hang over our lives.

Let there be no doubt that we are confused about our bodies and about how to nourish ourselves properly. Experts at the University of North Carolina have found that three-quarters of all American women have disordered feelings, thoughts, and behaviors related to eating. In the struggle to get or stay thin we skip meals, smoke cigarettes, and cut back to as little as a few hundred calories per day. One in three women have practiced purging with the use of laxatives or by making themselves vomit up food. Even the first season winner of *The Biggest Loser*, who was once considered a paragon of sensible weight-loss success, admitted he made himself so dehydrated that during the contest he passed blood in his urine. (This champion, Ryan Benson, also gained back almost all of the weight he lost.) On the other side of the disorder spectrum, many of us cannot tell when we are physically hungry or, once we begin to eat, when we have had enough.

Some of the blame for our problems with food should be assumed by the industries that produce and sell what we eat and by the officials who regulate them. Together they have sweetened and supersized the American diet to the point where people become addicted to overprocessed foods and have trouble even finding healthy alternatives. But as I consider my own attempts to manage weight and food and what I have discovered in my research and my psychotherapy practice, I have to conclude that the phobic response we have to weight as a sign of ugliness is a far more potent factor when it comes our feelings, actions, and relationship to food. Our fear of ugliness hovers over and adds a level of emotion to eating that can create confusion and anxiety that make it difficult to think clearly.

As Professor Hesse-Biber points out, the culture has established a remorseless system of punishments and rewards for women (and, increasingly, men) based on one's ability to achieve and maintain a slim physique. Time and nature, which tend to make every one of us fill out, combine with other factors (the unhealthy food supply, stressed-out lifestyles, consumerism, and so on) to make success practically impossible. As a result of this terrible dynamic, most of us have what I call a "failure script" that echoes in our minds throughout the day, making it that much more difficult to function. The script varies from person to person. But in general it warns us that nobody knows how to get or stay slim without a severely restrictive diet and an exercise regime that takes so much time there's hardly room for anything else. The script also tells us that since appearance matters more than anything else, our failure in this department will make us failures at everything. In fact, it can even lead us to believe that we are failures as human beings, and unworthy of love, attention, or self-respect.

And yet we keep trying, making annual New Year's resolutions, enrolling in weight-loss programs, and buying gym memberships. Sales of diet books, programs, and special foods remain strong whatever the economic climate, and "celebrity secrets" for taking off pounds remain a staple of the mass media. We pop pills, gulp caffeine, and cut calories to the point where we sometimes simply keel over from undernourishment. (In 2007, the New York Metropolitan Transit Authority reported that "sick customer" incidents, the number-three cause of subway service disruptions, typically involve women who faint during the morning rush to work due to crash diets.) Among my psychotherapy clients, who come from a fairly typical cross section of American life, weight and food are a source of constant worry and confusion, and genuine eating disorders like anorexia (compulsive severe dieting) and bulimia (binging and then purging) are not uncommon. We spend quite a bit of time exploring the origins of these problems and can usually identify ways that they were taught, by their families and the larger society, to become phobic about fat and obsessed with controlling their food intake. Beneath some of this behavior may be the belief that "I'm not worthy of being fed unless I'm perfect." In other cases people begin by trying to comply with the cultural imperative to "eat healthier." In nearly all, asserting power over the body and food intake brings temporary relief from appearance-based anxiety.

If your fear of fat seems to be controlled when you don't eat, and then you receive praise for losing weight—"You look terrific!"—then disordered eating starts to make sense as an antidote to ugliphobia. One anorexic teenager I treated loved getting admiration from others for "how hard she works" to stay thin. The smaller she got, the more she resembled television and movie stars, and the more she was praised for this achievement. Because she knew that others might be concerned that she was feeling pressured to diet, she tried to avoid going too far with her weight-loss effort and said things like "This is for me" when people asked why she was working so hard at it.

However, as psychotherapist and spiritual scholar Anthony de Mello wrote, the moment you renounce something (like food), you become tied to it even more tightly. Anorexics and bulimics may think they have succeeded in their battle with food and weight but in fact they have made these issues even more intense. Many, like my young client, keep their obsession going with the aid of so-called "pro-ana" websites, where people with eating disorders offer each other support and tips on how to get thin and stay thin.

When I looked at my client's favorite website, I saw contributors who called themselves things like: bonesrbeautiful, nothing, obesophobia, howtodisappear, and have2Bthinner. They were mostly female, of all different ages, and were writing from all over the world. Among the more popular slogans on the site was, "Nothing tastes as good as thin feels." Many of the posts dwelled on the idea that food actually contaminates the body, becoming (through the process of digestion) a filthy, foreign substance that must be removed as quickly and thoroughly as possible.

Anorexics who develop an obsession with "purifying" their bodies abuse laxatives and so-called "cleansing" regimens, which utilize enemas to "flush" the colon. Although no serious science supports the idea that we have dangerous toxins in our digestive systems that require attention, a large industry has emerged in the last two decades to promote this idea and deliver cleansing services to people who rely on them to lose weight and soothe the shame and anxiety they feel about their bodies being dirty, ugly, and perhaps even sinful. (We may not understand the religious/cultural background for why we worry about our bodies being impure, but we do feel the anxiety.)

The variety of disordered behavior related to food, weight, and the fear of ugliness includes at one end of the spectrum a basic confusion about when and how much to eat. (This is a problem I share with many women.) At the other end of the range are the exotic subgroups of anorexia, the so-called starving disease. These include "pregorexia" which involves starving yourself and your developing baby when you are pregnant, and diabulimia, which is practiced by diebetics who won't take their insulin in order to lose weight. Drunkorexics starve themselves to save calories so they can binge drink and not get fat. Beyond these food-related disorders are a host of appearance-related obsessions including the addictive use of tanning lights, which can contribute to the development of skin cancer.

One of the worst manifestations of our general confusion about our appearance arises when a person (almost always a girl or woman) loses the ability to recognize the size and shape of her own body. People who have body dysmorphic disorder (BDD) absorb and adopt our culture's tendency to objectify the body to the degree where they see only parts of themselves—a hip, an arm, a thigh—and are relentlessly critical in their evaluation of their condition. When asked to draw an outline of their bodies, women with BDD invariably produce a figure that is grossly distorted, and, when confronted by the true outline of their bodies, they refuse to believe that the smaller drawing represents reality.

Hard data on the incidence of BDD and other eating disorders is difficult to come by, but the best meta-analyses of the research show that since 1980 they have all risen in tandem with the proliferation of the mass media and the steady slimming of the female body ideal. Although disordered eating has been seen in other time periods—anorexia was first named by the Victorians who favored the "tubercular" look—the problem is more widespread and severe in our modern age.

Anorexia, which is glamorized in the media, cuts across income groups and regions and affects increasing numbers of people in groups once considered almost immune, such as African American women and white males. Second-generation Hispanic American women, who identify strongly with the mainstream culture in the United States, seem to be especially susceptible. It can also be seen in a related phenomenon called "heroin chic." This "look," which is featured in fashion advertising, depends on hollow-eyed models who are so pale and thin that they look sick.

Rising wealth and the spread of Western media and beauty standards appear to be spreading the problem of eating disorders to Eastern Europe and to parts of Asia, the Middle East, and South America. If the rise of fat obsession in these countries isn't proof that culture drives the fear of ugliness and its associated problems, consider the experience of women in Western Fiji.

For centuries Fijian life revolved around food. People beckoned passersby to join in feasts that demonstrated their wealth. Big women were considered beautiful and eating disorders were unknown. Then, in 1995, came television and programs from America showing, among other things, the benefits enjoyed by female characters who look like the Hollywood ideal. By 1998 more than ten percent of the Fijian girls surveyed by Harvard University Medical School psychiatrist Anne Becker reported purging at least once in order to lose weight. Referring to Western actresses she had seen, one girl explained, "I want their body, I want their size."

Although television brought other social problems, including sudden demand for consumer goods that most Fijians couldn't afford, the medium's effect on young women and their self-image was most startling. They came to think of themselves as "poor and fat," noted Becker, and they also yearned for a future that included a wealthy, urban lifestyle. In 2007 Becker studied more than five hundred Fijian females of high school age and discovered 45 percent had purged within the last month. But paradoxically, many also used appetite stimulants so they could eat like traditional Fijians and make their elders happy.

The plight of the TV-watching women in Fiji shows, in microcosm, the sociogenic power of media images. Even though the actresses they saw on the screen were mainly white women living in settings that couldn't have been more foreign, they still got the message that beauty and slimness equaled success. Thanks to media, the emotional contagion of ugliphobia had struck without them even having regular contact with living people who could model the fear and the struggle. (This phenomenon was a mass case of trauma by proxy.) Unfortunately, if the experience of their sisters in Western developed countries tells us anything about the future for the young women of Fiji, more trouble lies ahead.

12

ACTS OF DESPERATION

"Oh, that way madness lies; let me shun that."

—William Shakespeare (King Lear)

When Anne Becker explored the context of eating disorders in Fiji she discovered one additional disturbing fact: the mothers of the young women who were determined to look like the stars on TV shared their daughters' ambitions. They hoped that if their children became Western-style beauties they might be able to leave the South Pacific and a life that they had learned to regard as impoverished and isolated.

No relationship in life is more important, especially when it comes to shaping our self-concept, personality, and character, than the one shared by a mother and child. In a mother's eyes, a child sees her first reflection of herself and gets a sense of her true value. Unfortunately, parents, who have a documented tendency to favor children who fit the culturally established definition for attractiveness, often make a child's weight, hair, posture, or other physical features an issue for constant criticism or even discipline. Their faces reflect for their child a love mixed with disappointment, anxiety, and fear.

Most parents who pressure a child about appearance would say that they are trying to help a child become a success in the future. However, I believe that on a deeper and usually unconscious level, parents who focus intently on how a child looks are projecting their own ugliphobia and passing the hot potato of shame to the next generation. Typical is a story that one younger member of a worldwide Internet forum for women (I served as administrator for much of 2009) told me about the time she spends hiking with her mother. In what otherwise might be a perfect time for closeness, this young woman's mom couldn't help explaining that daughter's post-hike fatigue is caused by the fact that she is "unfit." She makes this comment every time they go walking, and it hurts her daughter, every time.

In worse cases, parents conduct running conflicts with their kids over food, exercise, fashion, and other issues related to their child's appearance. The net effect of such concerted effort to "save" a child from being ugly is to ensure that she becomes a woman who has internalized this obsession and always judges herself negatively. One woman on the All Facebook Females Unite in One Group forum recalled recently that she was identified as "the fattest daughter" at a holiday get-together. She was so upset that she made sure that her sister erased her from the photo taken at the gathering. (Photos are a particular problem for people who feel they are ugly and are constantly scanning their environment to avoid humiliation. If their anxiety is related to their size they may also be wary of restaurants, where people watch what they eat, and airplanes with small seats.)

When we feel like we would like to delete or erase ourselves, those inclined to be hostile and controlling sense our low self-regard, and are more likely to target us for abuse. In many cases of sexual harassment or sexual assault, the perpetrator says the victim was ugly and either deserved what she got or actually welcomed the attention because she couldn't otherwise attract anyone's interest. In my practice I have worked with a young woman who was sexually abused at age fourteen by a man who later said, "I'd fuck her again, if she lost twenty pounds. If she lost forty, I'd do it with my eyes open." The inference—that the victim was

ugly and therefore deserved her fate—was obvious. So was the perpetrator's attempt to project his guilt and shame onto her. This is common
practice as ugliness is seen by many as a justification, if not an invitation,
for cruel and even violent behavior.

Sexual assaults are not inevitable when you are raised to believe you
are ugly, but experience teaches most of us that ugly people face not only
limited opportunities but danger in the form of harassment and abuse.
We naturally fear this fate and try everything we can—diets, new fashions, hair care, makeup—to win approval and acceptance. If all of this
fails and we still hear from others that we are ugly, or can't quiet the inner
voice of judgment and worry, we can take dramatic action that involves
risking, quite literally, our lives for the sake of beauty.

Like everyone else, my decision to undergo plastic surgery—eyes, forehead, and neck—was driven by the realization that there was nothing
more I could do myself to look a little younger and that a surgeon could
give me an advantage I might need. I was looking forward to the publication of my first book and worrying about making public appearances.
First-time authors who want to keep on writing books need to sell
enough copies to encourage publishers to give them a second chance. I
walked up and down the aisles at bookstores and noticed that many of
the big sellers featured cover photos of people who looked younger and
more conventionally beautiful than me. The more I thought about my
age (I was pushing fifty) and the value our society places on beauty, the
more worried I became about whether people would buy a book written
by someone who looked like me.

There was a time, before author photos appeared on every book,
when a writer's appearance mattered little. And I know, in my logical
mind, that the way someone looks shouldn't affect a reader's decision

about what she writes. But in my heart I believed I was facing the same kind of challenge—a competition for scarce resources—that human beings have pursued from the beginning of time. For women this scramble was traditionally organized around winning the love and loyalty of a man who would provide protection and support for themselves and their children. This was especially true when societies were less developed and survival depended on our own physical efforts. In modern times women may be able to provide for their own well-being, but biology and culture still motivate us to seek success in part through beauty.

The beauty-equals-success paradigm is most alive in the media. As I prepared for my book to be published I knew I was about to plunge into the world of TV cameras, bright lights, and interviews. Afraid of being judged, and afraid that it was not enough for me to write a good book, I even started to worry that my appearance would actually discourage people from considering what I had to say. After what I *thought* was careful consideration of all the issues, I consulted a surgeon. This first step trapped me in an almost irreconcilable conflict.

The doctor I saw was a warm and self-confident man who smiled a lot and listened carefully. When it came time for him to assess my face he broke it down into parts—eyes, neck, chin, forehead, and so on—and seemed to talk about them objectively, like he was checking out a used car. This act of dis-integrating my body from myself made it easier for us to recognize "problems" and discuss what needed to be "fixed" in a detached and almost clinical way. By the time we were finished comparing my various parts to the ideal he might produce with a scalpel, I felt like it was quite reasonable to let him slice apart my face and to pay him well for the service.

After I left the office, where I had made an almost-final decision to go ahead with surgery, I immediately began to reconsider. Although I had chosen this physician with great care, checking his record on state databases that charted complaints and malpractice cases, and getting personal referrals, I knew that all operations come with risk. If I went forward I faced possible complications like infection, scarring, and even blindness. Then there were the mishaps that can come with anesthesia. An accident or allergic reaction can cause brain damage and even death. Finally there was the values statement I would make with the choice. How would I explain to my two daughters, whom I had taught to love themselves just as they are, that I was going "under the knife"?

Caught between the reasonable idea that I should avail myself of a common tool for "self-improvement" and the risks this option posed to my life, limb, and self-image, I felt completely confused. Would I be a pathetic, superficial, and hypocritical person if I chose the surgery? Or would I be pathetic, self-defeating, and shortsighted if I didn't? Finally I decided that the potential benefits outweighed the risks and that I should have the surgery. I would consider it an "investment" in my professional future. With much anxiety I scheduled an appointment in the operating suite, took time off from work for my recovery, and surrendered myself to the surgeon's care.

From the moment I awoke after the operation I regretted taking the risk with my life and the worry my choice caused my supportive husband and children. As I write this, news outlets are reporting on the funeral and burial services for one-time Miss Argentina Solange Magnano, a thirty-eight year old who died of complications from a procedure that was supposed to make her buttocks rounder and firmer. Her death, in a country known as a mecca for cosmetic surgery, where even the poor have "work" done, prompted an outpouring of concerns for her twin children but no apparent decline in demand for body-sculpting operations.

My recovery from facial surgery was slow and painful and became quite complicated when fluid pooled in my neck making it look like I had a rope wrapped around my throat. (In retrospect, the noose-like shape of the swelling was quite ironic.) I wore turtlenecks and went for post-op care—the doctor drew blood out of the swollen tissue with a big syringe—

half a dozen times before this complication subsided. The drive to the doctor's office and waiting room time allowed me to reflect and consider what I had done. The scales tipped in favor of regret when the doctor told me with pride, "You have the jaw line of a seventeen-year-old." He didn't know that minutes before I had overheard him tell a patient in the next room, "You have the breasts of a seventeen-year-old."

In the years since the surgery, my first book did well enough for me to continue writing; it was impossible to tell what effect my appearance had on whether readers bought it or not. I eventually concluded that before the surgery I had been so influenced by cultural messages and my own ugliphobia that I couldn't even make an accurate assessment in the mirror. It was as if I had body dysmorphic disorder (something I fear most women suffer) and saw myself through a filter of worry that got worse with the prospect of public appearances and media attention.

Given the chance to go back and make the choice without so much fear, I know I would forego the surgery. But having done it, I am glad for the insight and empathy it has helped me develop for myself and everyone else who opts for a cosmetic procedure. Counting collagen injections and laser hair removal, American medical offices deliver about 12 million cosmetic services annually. The amount people invest in these procedures is more than $12 billion, and the most popular operations are, in order, breast augmentation, liposuction, nose jobs, eyelid surgery, and tummy tucks.

The explosive growth of plastic surgery in America and around the world has been thoroughly examined by historians and social scientists who note that technology has continually expanded our ability to reshape our physical selves. Every year seems to bring new types of operations and other medically styled ways to change our appearance or intervene in the aging process. Normal aging is being redefined as a malady to be treated medically. In most American cities you can find the equivalent of the Miami Institute of Age Management & Intervention (MIAMI), a center staffed by doctors and nurses that offers more than a dozen plastic surgery procedures.

In my imagination, places like this will eventually offer surgeries and treatments that will give adult women the appearance of little children. This fantasy is not as wild as it may seem. The ideal human face of today has wide eyes, smooth skin, and a small nose, just like a baby's face. (This is true across cultures, as evidenced by a spate of recent news reports describing Iran as the nose-reduction capital of the world.) When animals like the "toy" breeds of certain dogs retain such juvenile characteristics, biologists call the phenomenon "neoteny" (similar to the word neonate). I think our cultural obsession with youth is a kind of social neoteny that puts pressure on women to not just erase any sign that they have given birth, but also to look as innocent and helpless as children. The psychological implications of neoteny are quite profound, especially when you consider that the same women who have their faces "rejuvenated" to the point of looking childlike are also supposed to have substantial adult sexual characteristics—big breasts, rounded buttocks, puffed-up lips that signal arousal—that may also be supplied through surgery.

Although plastic surgery and other big anti-aging "interventions" are often presented as routine, they all have deep psychological meaning. For example, surgeons now remove parts of toes so that women can fit into certain designer shoes. On one level this can be seen as a modern version of Chinese foot binding, which makes a woman physically delicate and vulnerable. On another level, elective toe amputation allows a woman to fit into and deploy—as objects of fashion, beauty, and power—designer shoes that signal her high status. Seen this way, the surgery may be considered both a symbol of ugliphobia and an adaptation to social standards.

I see the same duality in the increasingly popular "mommy makeover," which involves a tummy tuck, liposuction, and breast lift/augmentation. Intended to restore the body to its pre-pregnancy condition, this surgical package regards the physical effects of having a baby as a kind of disease. (This is, in part, an extension of the cultural shift that made childbirth a highly medicalized event that began when birth was moved from the home to hospitals.) The impulse behind the mommy makeover is both modern and primal. It is modern because it involves surgical equipment and techniques which are, forgive the pun, cutting-edge. How else could they make such an assault on the body and yet deliver you home on the same day? The mommy makeover is also primal because it emphasizes a woman's value as a fresh, never-been-used vessel for reproduction. As a mommy you have obviously had sex and are therefore less desirable. After a makeover, you can look like you haven't had sex and thus become a MILF, slang for the term *mother I'd like to fuck.*

The value of virginity, and hence MILF status, goes back to ancient Rome—remember the vestal virgins?—and beyond. I imagine that many patients who choose this whole-body surgical revision believe it will make them more desirable to their partners or others, and that by increasing their physical appeal they make themselves somehow more secure and even powerful.

The variety of surgeries, chemical applications, laser treatments, and injections offered by medical practitioners is so broad and ever changing that it's impossible to offer a comprehensive list here. Americans now spend more than $1 billion per year on injections of paralyzing botulinum toxins (the trademarked product is called Botox) to smooth wrinkles, and roughly three times as much on cosmetic dentistry. (Everyone now wants teeth as perfectly aligned and white as the ones they see on TV and film, which may explain why 80 percent of people surveyed by the American Dental Association are unhappy with their smiles.)

Teeth whiteners are relatively inexpensive, which means almost anyone can get on the cosmetic dentistry bandwagon, but if you think that more expensive procedures like breast enhancements and liposuction are only for the rich, think again. The American Society of Plastic surgeons say that 60 percent of their patients earn less than $90,000. People looking for a bargain can turn to physicians who are not board-certified and perform these operations at low prices. One patient in my therapy practice (a man) actually drove to a general practitioner's office on a Saturday afternoon for liposuction to remove "love handles" that I couldn't see. The operation was performed under local anesthesia, and after binding the incisions, the doctor drove him home.

Medical options become an active choice when we feel we have exhausted diet and exercise and just cannot get the look we think we should have. Many of the businesses that have sprung up to meet the demand for these services market themselves as "medi-spas" and "institutes" similar to places where you might get a massage or a special treatment to exfoliate your pores. Their waiting rooms are filled with beautiful images of happy men and women who presumably look younger than their years, and consultations for services focus on the benefits that come with getting a more ideal look. If you care to read the fine print, as I did, you learn that, "Breast implants are not lifetime devices, and breast implantation is likely not a one-time surgery. You may need additional unplanned surgeries on your breasts because of complications or unacceptable cosmetic outcomes."

Similar disclaimers are offered for every procedure, but it's hard to imagine that potential patients devote much time to the warnings. (I didn't, until after my surgery when I heard that novelist Olivia Goldsmith, author of *The First Wives Club*, died of complications from anesthesia administered for a procedure like the one I had.) Cosmetic surgery is so commonplace that even many of the dolls we give to little girls look like they have had their bodies and faces surgically enhanced. Plastic surgery gets so much media attention that any well-read person would believe he knows all about it. We all know the "success" stories common on TV "makeover" programs, which often feature people who have many different parts of their bodies—teeth, face, breasts, skin—altered so they can go out into the world with confidence. Most episodes end with the lucky beneficiary dressed in a new wardrobe with her hair cut stylishly and makeup perfectly applied, being greeted by family and friends to her new life. Everyone weeps with pride and joy.

The TV shows make it seem like even the ugliest among us can find happiness if only we change our appearance. (They are so popular that in 2010 a home-shopping channel actually declared May 20 "National Makeover Day" and announced plans for it to be an annual event.) The idea that we can be instantly "made over" makes some people desperate for quick and dramatic ways to change their appearance and has contributed to the growth of a black market occupied by doctors who perform cosmetic procedures without proper certification and others who have no medical licenses at all. Some of these entrepreneurs offer real services and products like Botox and medical grade silicone. Others have actually disfigured and even killed people, injecting substances such as castor oil, mineral oil, petroleum jelly, and automobile transmission fluid, and claiming they were filling in facial lines and wrinkles.

Though real, the criminal and just plain incompetent practices found at the margins of the cosmetic surgery business are true exceptions, and a careful consumer can separate the reputable providers from the dangerous ones. But even after you assure yourself that you are in competent hands, you still have to ask whether an extreme option like cosmetic surgery will deliver the result you want.

The surgeons themselves will echo the makeover TV programs and emphasize the positive feelings many people experience when they see that they look more like the cultural ideal. And many women will argue that these operations can actually be empowering for those who make a conscious choice to sculpt their bodies for their own reasons. If the body and its parts are commodities, why shouldn't we own them and do with them as we please? Beauty can be powerful, and from the very beginning of modern cosmetic surgery, patients reported that a new nose or tighter skin left them feeling happier and more confident. Many poorer women believe their chances for moving up the economic ladder—through marriage or their own careers—can be improved through cosmetic procedures, and they take out long-term loans to get them.

Few long-term studies have been done to chart the quality of life for people who have had breast augmentation, liposuction, tummy tucks, and facelifts. Many people consider the choice to have these types of surgery a very private matter, and it would be difficult to persuade a large number to talk about their experience. (As the Maybelline cosmetics jingle—"Maybe she's born with it, maybe it's Maybelline."—reminds us, a woman is supposed to look as if she came by her beauty effortlessly and naturally.) Among the women I know who have had surgery to change their appearance, most came away satisfied. The happiest was a therapy client who had bariatric surgery and subsequently lost almost one hundred pounds. She said that the best thing about this change was the way that it freed her from negative feelings about her size. Less self-conscious and self-critical, she reported that she was just nicer to be around and had more positive experiences going through her daily life.

The little scientific data available about the psychological effects of plastic surgery also suggests that most people are happy with what they get, so long as they don't suffer significant complications. One large study reported in a journal for plastic surgery nurses found that after a year, most breast augmentation patients were happy with the results.

Several research teams have been able to follow rhinoplasty (nose job) patients for as long as five years. These studies found a lasting and significant rise in self-esteem and sociability in these patients. They didn't experience dramatic changes when it came to serious mental health issues. Those with problems still had problems. But they seem to have a better outlook on life overall.

The rhinoplasty results are not surprising when you consider that it may be the only one-time plastic surgery procedure that results in a substantial change that lasts a lifetime. With almost every other option, whatever has been tightened or plumped up by a doctor is going to age, wrinkle, sag, or get fat again. When this happens, a new decision must be made. Will you keep up the technological fight against time and gravity, or will you accept nature's course? Most people seek a middle ground, and eventually accept the effects of time. A few, however, become, for lack of a better term, surgery addicts. Once they have the perfect nose they have to have the perfect chin, and then the perfect breasts and buttocks. By the time they are finished working over their bodies, time has taken its toll and they start all over again.

No one should tell anyone what to do when it comes to their body. Millions of people have undergone cosmetic procedures and felt they benefited from them. And for every sobering story of death and injury that appears in the press, the proponents of plastic surgery can point to many lives that have been improved. As many in the profession say, even those who seek operations for flaws that no one else can see are sometimes helped, psychologically, by the process of addressing their perceived problem. I imagine these operations as effective placebos.

As a response to the cultural standards for beauty, which we cannot help but internalize, any one of the medical options can provide at least a modicum of relief. The only point I would stress, based on my experience as a patient, my research, and my work as a psychotherapist, is that we should all consider the factors that can push us toward the surgeon's office. Do we view our bodies in a clear-eyed way? Could the discomfort we feel about our appearance actually be a diversion from some other problem—depression, anxiety, loneliness—that could be addressed in a different way? Are we trying to measure up to a media-based standard for appearance that, thanks to technology, represents something beyond what a natural human being can achieve? Are there limits to your pursuit of perfection?

The key to making a good decision, one that you can be happy with, seems to lie in understanding all the forces behind both the large-scale boom in cosmetic medicine and our choices as individuals. Here I think most of us fall short. A startling example of this gap between understanding and action arose in my office recently when a mother came to see me with her teenage daughter who wanted surgery on her labia to make them smaller. This operation is becoming so popular that some surgeons who perform it actually advertise for patients/customers. Michael Safir, M.D., of Beverly Hills sells his labial reduction surgery to readers of *LA Weekly* with promises of "affordable, exceptional care" and free parking.

With a little talking, my psychotherapy patient and her mother realized that her desire for labial reconstruction had been affected, at least in part, by images of women in pornography. After a discussion of airbrushing, Photoshop, and the porn world's obsession with youthful-looking body parts, my patient's problem seemed far less urgent to her. She still worried that anyone who saw her naked, including future sexual partners, might find her ugly or tease her, but she did feel more comfortable waiting to see how she thought about it in a few years.

13

HATRED IN ACTION

"I feel ugly most of the time. This probably sounds silly, but I never used to. I used to think I was okay. But, I started to put weight on a couple of years ago and my so-called 'boyfriend' (lol) has made loads of comments, so much so that I just want to hide."

—D. K., Manchester, England

"It is really ironic that as a thin pretty teenager I felt very fat and ugly due to the abuse of my father, who used to call me fat ass, etc."

—L. C., New York

"When I was in high school and younger I was picked on and bullied and ignored by the guys. I hated to look at myself in the mirror. HATED it."

—C. R., Toronto

When I began exploring the topic of ugliness on the million-plus-member Facebook women's forum, the initial responses revealed that worries about being ugly and the fear of isolation and loneliness that ugliness implies are practically universal. My opening question—*When do you feel ugly?*—invited this kind of reply because it didn't ask women if they wanted to confront the ugliness issue in themselves. Instead it just gave them permission to share their experiences.

As a dialogue developed, I came to see that the anxiety and ambivalence so many bring to the mirror each day matched the fearful response that a child may have when he has to encounter a chronically abusive parent at home or a tormenter at school. In fact, many women actually felt bullied when it came to the matter of their appearance, and more than a few had experienced bullying in family relationships. These bullies depend on an imbalance of power to exert unwanted influence and control. Their aggression can be verbal—name-calling, criticism, threats—physical, and social. (Bullies often try to exclude their targets from social groups, lie about them, or spread rumors.)

This abusive behavior can take place almost anywhere and is increasingly common in the online world of cyberspace. Perpetrators may act to exercise power and thereby exorcise their own feelings of powerlessness, or because they get reinforcement from a group. When it comes to the matter of ugliness, we meet bullies in every corner of society, from our personal lives to the broader social marketplace where we are constantly hectored to do, buy, try something—anything!—to protect ourselves from our own hideousness.

A person who is bullied becomes frightened, tentative, self-doubting, and, eventually, self-critical. This is precisely how many of us act when we consider our own appearance, and it's hard to escape these feelings because we live at a time when bullying, by perpetrators who call others ugly, has reached epidemic proportions.

Though not a formal survey, my Facebook post prompted many accounts by women, men, and children who have been bullied about their weight, their figures, their height, and even faces. A startling number of male and female children are hounded by both parents and siblings who routinely call them "lard ass" or "wide load" as well as the time-honored "pig," "fatty," "ugly," and "dog."

Hardly anyone alive has escaped this kind of name-calling, but it hurts much more when it is repetitive and when the source is someone who is supposed to have your best interest at heart. In some circumstances a bullying parent (for example) actually believes that she is helping a child with doses of "tough love" that will motivate the child to lose weight, exercise, or make some change in wardrobe or appearance in order to comply with social norms. Pathologically abusive parents will use a child's supposed ugliness as a justification for violent and sexual assaults.

More careful mothers and fathers might forego the violent language while still delivering the same kinds of bullying messages in sugar-coated form. When this occurs, a mother might repeatedly say, "You don't want to wind up like [insert the name of an unhappy "ugly" person here] do you?" A father using this strategy could constantly remind his son that successful men project a certain kind of appearance—straight-backed, muscular, neatly turned-out—and point to boys who, unlike his own son, clearly comply with the norm.

Whether it's done directly—"you fat slob"—or indirectly—"Why don't you dress like your sister?"—appearance-based bullying rarely works the way a parent hopes it will, and, more typically, it leads a child to fear or even hate the perpetrator. Of course, a young child's developing psyche cannot allow for the conscious rejection of a parent who represents love, safety, and survival to him. Almost always these feelings are relegated to the subconscious where they are sometimes converted into self-hatred or just quietly erode a child's sense of self-esteem and safety. If you wonder why so many people feel ugly at the moment when they awaken and are least guarded, psychologically, the experience of being bullied by an internalized parental voice is one plausible explanation.

Unfortunately, children who are bullied at home may have to face more of the same when they go out into the world. Playgrounds and schools can be breeding grounds for bullying behavior, as anyone who has been through junior high or middle school knows.

On Facebook, I heard from many people who had been verbally and physically abused by schoolmates and neighborhood kids who made a point of justifying their attack with the claim that their "ugly" victim deserved it. In the worst cases bullying cascades to the point of physical and sexual abuse. I had this experience myself as a girl, when boys who deemed it perfectly reasonable to repeatedly mock me as a "dog" finally egged each other on until they had me pinned and could grope me. This kind of incident, depends, in part, on the group dynamics that arise when a bully takes control, and others who fear being targeted themselves both join in and amplify the abuse. You can also see this fear at work when, as a bully attacks, otherwise kind people hang back and fail to come to the victim's defense. This experience of falling short of your own values can produce long-lasting guilt and regret as one Facebook correspondent confessed:

> I got bullied a lot. What I find myself feeling guilty about as an adult is that there were other girls who were also bullied that I liked and wanted to be friends with. I would hang out with them in "private" but would shun them in "public" for fear of receiving even worse bullying just for hanging out with that person. I do regret those actions and I suppose one could call that "passive bullying."

This writer received an outpouring of online support from people who admired her honesty and confessed that they, too, had stood in silence when children who fell short of some social standard for appearance were bullied. During this lively discussion, which went on for days, it became clear that many people had continued to reflect on the problem of shunning and bullying long into their adult lives. One member of the forum who worked with children said, "It's very interesting to watch young girls playing in the school playground. As young as seven years old you can pick out the leaders and the followers. These little girls start out at a very young age bullying their fellow playmates."

We've all seen this happen. A group of children follow a leader who selects an overweight or unfashionably dressed victim for humiliation. They may pretend to accept her, then suddenly turn and mock, or they might just hurl insults until their target can no longer ignore them. Sadly, young people can be remarkably creative as they express this kind of hostility. Victims are often at a loss to respond, and the main option for maintaining one's dignity in these circumstances is to pretend that the attacks don't matter.

Adult observers, like my Facebook contributor, may recall their own experiences or struggle to make sense of a bully's behavior. "It's also interesting that when following these girls through to adulthood, their tendency to bully continues," she wrote. "I do believe that it's in their nature to be controlling. A lot of parents are shocked when they discover that it's their child that's the bully."

From my perspective, the tendency to bully those who don't conform is hardly surprising given how common this practice can be in families and the bullying quality of our culture. Whether you consider the arts, media, or commerce, we are constantly pressured to meet the beauty ideal, and we know the punishment that can be visited upon us. The most pernicious actors in this dynamic are corporations that market anxiety and fear to sell products. Huge swathes of the fashion, cosmetic, and personal-care product industries fall into this category as they use both subtle and high-pressure techniques to bully us to buy whatever they sell in order to avoid the fate of rejection, loneliness, and failure.

I don't mean to say that no one should express her creativity through fashion or the artistry of makeup or other forms of styling. And I certainly understand that our lives depend on commerce. What I am saying is that as sales-hungry companies push for higher profits, some of them turn to techniques that prey on our insecurities. The woman who doesn't buy the right shampoo, makeup, or bra is generally portrayed as less beautiful than the one who does, and her fate, at least as far as can be determined in the advertisement, is always less pleasant.

To take an extremely obvious example, which I noted earlier in this book, Sharon Osbourne was the main bully who organized a small group— the morning radio show hosts—to go after the singer Susan Boyle in the fall of 2009. (Osbourne could hardly claim to be unaware of the effect of her comment. *Before* she mocked Susan Boyle, Osbourne added her voice to those who objected to the designer Karl Lagerfeld's cruelly cavalier remarks about how those who worry about hyper-thin fashion models are "fat mummies sitting with their bags of crisps in front of the television.")

Ugly bullying abounds on the radio, perhaps because it's one medium that allows performers to make their attacks without being seen themselves. On any given day an alert radio listener might hear one host refer to Hillary Clinton as "her thighness," and another make fun of the appearance of the teenage pop star Miley Cyrus. Women, who are supposed to be always erotogenic, seem to draw the most attention from media bullies who focus on appearance, and this is especially true if the woman has power. In recent years this kind of bigotry has been aimed not only at Clinton but at Nancy Pelosi, speaker of the United States House of Representatives, one-time secretary of state Condoleezza Rice, and former attorney general Janet Reno. No matter your age, office, or place on the political spectrum, if you're a powerful woman certain people feel they have the right to criticize not just your performance but your appearance. You will be mocked if you're too tall, too heavy, too old, or too wrinkly. And of course, if you try to conform to the extreme beauty standards of the day and opt for plastic surgery, you'll be bullied for that too.

Men come in for radio bullying too. Before he died, Senator Ted Kennedy was the object of constant commentary about being overweight, and one of the main things Representative Dennis Kucinich is known for is his height. Fortunately for them, men are not scrutinized as closely as women, and their accomplishments appear to insulate them from attacks on their appearance. This may be why we're startled when we actually hear a bully target a powerful man. I'll never forget the outburst I heard while waiting on the phone to answer a radio talk show host's questions live on the air. Just before picking up the line to talk to me she ranted about former New York mayor Rudolph Giuliani's baldness and how his attempt to cover it with a "comb-over" was ludicrous and ugly. The man was a serious candidate for president and had led the city through the tragedy of the 9/11 attacks, but this host could only focus on his hair. Her attitude was especially ironic to me since the subject we then discussed together was my book *The Velveteen Principles*, which is primarily about kindness and empathy.

Beyond the realm of talk radio, which is the most obvious place to find broadcasting bullies, we can also see aggressive efforts to intimidate people on the basis of appearance in television, film, and print. Also, an astonishing amount of "cyberbullying" takes place online. Much of this behavior involves appearance-based attacks not against famous celebrities, but rather young people who wind up the targets of either an individual bully or a mob of e-mailers and texters who feel compelled to call them ugly. Cyberbullying creates one more way for people who feel frightened and vulnerable to pass the "hot potato of shame," but it is also a way for people who are aggressive or even sadistic to hurt others under the cloak of anonymity.

The widely reported hounding of teen Megan Meier, who eventually committed suicide, provides a tragic but typical view of the cyberbully phenomenon. Most of the insults thrown at Megan were about her being "ugly," "fat," and "a slut." This combination displays a common and cruel bigotry, one that holds that women who fall short of some cultural idea of beauty must be sexually promiscuous in order to escape loneliness and rejection. Megan Meier was so distraught by it that she killed herself. The world was shocked to discover that her tormentor was the mother of one of Megan's schoolmates operating under cover of a false identity.

More recently, the bullying-by-technology phenomenon took another turn with the rise of "sexting," which involves sending explicit photos and messages via cell phone. Sexting allows anyone to create sexual images, including pictures that make the body into a kind of commodity or status object, and distribute them. In our appearance-obsessed society young people have taken to this practice in a big way. According to an Associated Press poll done in 2009, more than 25 percent of teens have sexted. Young women were more likely than young men to send out nude photos of themselves. But as with so many of the methods we use to promote ourselves as beautiful or desirable, sexting comes with considerable risk. Photos meant for one person's eyes can find their way to others and may even be posted on the Internet where they might live forever.

In 2008, teen Jessica Logan "sexted" a photo of herself to her boyfriend. When the two ended their relationship he sent the picture to friends. Soon students in two different schools were sharing the photo, and Jessica became the subject of harassment. In her attempt to be appealing and beautiful according to the social norm, which now encourages young women to dress and present themselves in sexually provocative and pornified ways, she wound up being called a "slut," "whore," and "skank." As one particular group of students continually harassed her, Logan began staying home from school. She isolated herself from others and became depressed until, like Megan Meier, she committed suicide. Her father found her body with her cell phone nearby.

Suicides that follow bullying reveal the level of anguish we can feel when we are under continual attack and cannot find a way to make it stop. In 2008, researchers at Yale University documented the connection between bullying and suicide in thirteen different countries. From South

Korea to South Africa to the United States, young people who are bullied are up to nine times more likely to kill themselves than other children. The same study, done by two medical doctors, Young Shin Kim and Bennett Leventhal, discovered that bullies themselves are five times more likely to commit suicide. This finding about the vulnerability of bullies themselves points to the fact that bullying is a behavior that is passed from one generation to the next.

This was certainly what happened with Elena, an All Facebook Females Unite in One Group contributor from Australia, who sparked a long conversation when she confessed that she had bullied others when she was young. "Yes, unfortunately, I was a terrible bully," she wrote. "I used to make peoples lives hell! Of course I am filled with regret now but I cannot undo what was done. I run into people that I was cruel to, as I live in a small town, and I apologize but it still doesn't make me feel any better."

A member of Australia's indigenous minority, Elena dealt with plenty of appearance and race-based bigotry outside her community, which only compounded abuse she suffered inside it. "I was sexually abused as a small child, five years old, by my parents' friends," she wrote to me. "My parents are both alcoholics and as a result I was never cared for as a small child should be. I had no control over my own environment or safety so I supposed I found it almost empowering to take control of someone else." As she exerted control, Elena abused others both emotionally and physically. Some suffered injuries that required hospital care. As an adult Elena spent many years in counseling, and the therapy did help. She also writes that her children "have changed me because I would never want them to grow up with my attitudes, fears, or behaviors."

People who have experienced direct bullying and grappled with its effects successfully, like Elena, can grow in empathy for themselves and others once they understand what has happened. This is no easy task. It takes a great deal of courage to face how we have been abused and even more to consider the damage we have done to others. But when we can accomplish these tasks with compassion, we can start to live with less fear, less guilt, and less shame.

You might reflect on stories like Elena's and think, *Whew. I'm glad I wasn't bullied.* I would say, "Not so fast." Take the analysis one last step, and consider that every person who tries to navigate our ugliphobic culture has been bullied in a thousand small ways. Every person who is less than perfect has been ignored, put down, passed over, and shortchanged innumerable times based on appearance. Mere existence in our media-saturated world means that we are never far away from a reminder that life holds great rewards for the beautiful and deprivation for the ugly. You are being handed a failure script that predicts an awful outcome for your life—because you are ugly—that you cannot change. The idea that you are a failure because you are not beautiful can become generalized until you feel a vague sense of incompetence in most of your daily life, but you don't know why.

A lifetime of these experiences leaves us with many of the symptoms that experts in bullying say arise when a person has been hounded, abused, and denigrated over an extended period of time. Among the symptoms noted by the Center for Relationship Abuse Awareness are:

The inability to be spontaneous
Loss of confidence, enthusiasm, courage, and creativity
Belief that something is wrong with you
Self-doubt
Internalized critical voice
Feeling crazy
The desire to escape and "numb out"
Confusion

Extremely common, these emotions suggest that the culture we inhabit is actually abusive to us as individual human beings who deserve far more than to be judged by how we appear. Fighting against the bully, which is all around us, is very difficult. And if we don't receive enough positive regard and empathy to counteract it, we run the risk of internalizing all these messages and bullying ourselves. This phenomenon is similar to the Stockholm syndrome, which was identified by researchers who saw that prisoners often identify with their captors. It is what is actually happening when we roll over in the morning and feel ugly, or step in front of the mirror and begin to criticize ourselves. We are taking on the bully role and harassing ourselves for not meeting the impossible beauty standard that someone else created.

I have bullied myself on the basis of appearance—silently chastising, criticizing, and picking on flaws—more times than I can count. This behavior is not intentional, and it's not unusual. Most of us quietly berate ourselves this way, expressing the voice of the internalized bully. Some bear down even harder. They deny themselves friendships, travel, work opportunities, and other rewards because they believe they are too ugly and undeserving. I suspect that many people with eating disorders and people who cut and burn themselves may be engaged in bullying themselves because they feel ugly.

These feelings—and the absence of joy—are so strong and persistent that they come to define our reality. One case in point is a nineteen-year-old I know who thinks she is so ugly she has trouble leaving her house. Amanda had been bullied in the past and was afraid of it happening again. But she was also in the habit of abusing herself—criticizing her own appearance in the mirror and dwelling on her supposed flaws—mercilessly. This self-bullying was far more damaging than anything she was likely to experience if she went out to run errands or have some fun. However, the echoes of judgment in her own head made it difficult for her to venture forth.

Not everyone turns to isolation and self-criticism in response to bullying. I have seen some rather positive rebellion against the bullying society in people who dress or decorate their bodies in ways that show they refuse to be bound by stereotypes.

I suspect that some of these people who opt for "body art" or very unusual fashions and hair styles are making a stand against the bullying culture. But in other cases they may be caught in the dichotomy observed by Anthony de Mello, who noted that every time we renounce something, we bind ourselves to it. Does an extreme approach to fashion or makeup communicate resistance to the "appearance is everything" culture or does it say "Look at me"? I really don't know.

What I do know is that almost every one of us must find a way to cope with the threat of bullying born out of the intense insecurity, fear, and anxiety that are the hallmarks of ugliphobia. This is especially true for young people who can be intensely vulnerable to the lure of being a bully and the pain of being the bully's target.

Part Four:

OVERCOMING UGLIPHOBIA

14

FACING THE TRUTH

"Truth only reveals itself when one gives up all pre-conceived ideas."

—Shoseki

Prettiness is a snake oil cure.

The message we get from our families, communities, and institutions (great and small) is that if we only conform to the ideal we'll be safe, secure, loved—in short, happy. And so, at an ever-younger age, we start shaving, tweezing, spraying, coating, dyeing, and dressing in an attempt to cure our ugliness as if it's a disease. The trouble is that the prescription changes with every new season for the fashion industry or every issue of a women's magazine.

As advertising and marketing professors Mary C. Martin and James W. Gentry discovered in a study they did in the 1990s, children begin to be influenced by the beauty standard in elementary school, and it erodes self-esteem—especially for girls—throughout the rest of childhood and adolescence. Martin and Gentry noted that girls are far more likely to identify their bodies as a sign of their value to others and to feel like they fail to live up to a social ideal. They quote an aspiring model whose grasp of the baffling challenge posed by appearance is remarkably mature:

. . . as long as they are there, screaming at me from the television, glaring at me from magazines, I'm stuck in the model trap. Hate them first. Then grow to like them. Emulate them. Die to be like them. All the while praying this cycle will come to an end.

Unfortunately, the cycle does not end of its own accord. We don't "age out" of the comparing and worrying, and there is no point in life when society—as represented by our peers, the media, and the marketplace— decides to just let us be ourselves. As a member of the enormous and enormously influential "baby boom" generation, I have noticed how the role models from my peer group are always presented as younger, slimmer, and more perfect than anyone their age. These manufactured beauties are then promoted to encourage us to be "Fabulous at Forty" or "Fantastic at Fifty" or "Sexy at Sixty." Their smiles tell us that they are reaping the rewards of all the time, effort, and expense they devote to maintaining the ideal and beckon us to learn their secrets and buy into the practices and products that win them these results.

Gazing at the newsstand or television, you may find yourself wondering, *When do I get a break from all of this? When will it be okay to just be myself?* The answer will never come from the mass media. Their business formula requires them to ignore the realities of time and nature and all the social factors that conspire to make us dissatisfied with ourselves. Instead they must make us feel individually responsible for our status as beautiful or ugly. It is then up to us to make our own bargain with the system, deciding just how much we'll invest—American women spend over $1 million per hour on cosmetics—in order to "pass."

The word "pass" is key because it recalls the strategies the people who belong to racial or ethnic minority groups have used in the past to appear to be in the majority and thus escape discrimination. In the United States some African Americans, for example, once used skin bleach, hair-straighteners, and other methods to appear "white" and evade discrimination. The effect of this effort on one's psyche can be profoundly painful. After all, "passing" requires that you renounce yourself and your origins in order to join the very group that oppresses you. Imagine the ethical implications of making the choice to pass, and accepting the benefits that are denied to others who may even be your brothers or sisters. Or consider the alternative. What if by deciding to forego the opportunity to join the majority you lose income, status, and other opportunities? Wouldn't you always wonder what you gave up?

Strange as it seems, every woman born into modern society is made to feel like part of an "out group" because she possesses physical characteristics that, while normal and universal, are also deemed "ugly." All women sprout hair on their legs and armpits and, eventually, on their chins and upper lips. We all get blemishes and gray hair. Our waists thicken, and our breasts droop. None of this happens to make-believe ideal women who are part of the "in-group" that is never ugly. Instead they are liposuctioned and coated with makeup, and then their images are Photoshopped to the point where they cannot recognize themselves.

And that's the problem. Even if you try to pass you never will. You can buy everything from the right underwear to a facelift and you will never be perfect. Indeed, if you go just a hair too far and wind up looking too artificial, then you will be considered ugly and pathetic for having tried too hard. This occurs because the rules are set so that something about you will always be ugly. And all the promises we are told about being pretty—beginning with the idea that beauty can be narrowly defined—are patently false.

Since no one and no "thing" is going to free us from ugliphobia (too much of our economy depends on it), the task falls to us as individuals. I think it helps to start by naming and rejecting the concepts—call them the Rules of Ugliphobia—that are used to shame us. Among the big ones are:

Your value depends on your appearance.

Some people are physically ugly.

Their ugliness merits disgust and rejection.

Beauty can be defined in a narrow way (think thin, young, Western European).

Conformity equals success and happiness.

Nonconformity leads to loneliness, unhappiness, irrelevance.

Each of these statements is true in certain contexts. If you want to join a snobby clique in high school or win the Miss Universe pageant—and your sense of self-worth depends on this kind of achievement—then of course you must pursue conventional beauty and conform to the ideal. But it's vital that we make conscious choices and distinguish between behaviors based on fear or compulsive conformity, and choices we make in a deliberate way in order to build a happy, creative, meaningful life.

Ask yourself if the effort you put into your outsides produces an image that matches you inside. I, for example, am a middle-aged, quirky, unathletic woman who values creativity, connection, and intelligence. Like most women I was often anxious about my appearance and could be quite self-critical. But I am also a person who doesn't let unresolved problems remain unresolved. I could feel the conflict between what I truly value and the way I sometimes tortured myself over my appearance.

Over time I began to challenge myself every time I noticed I had fallen into the habit of self-criticism. Also, as I grew older and the goal of looking young and conventionally beautiful became even harder to reach, I recognized that if I was ever going to find peace, I would have accept how I looked. Then, one day, it happened. I was in the middle of berating myself for being unfit and realized that I happen to look like what I am.

With my glasses and gray hair and soft body, I look like a woman who is not an avid young exerciser or sportsperson but just might be a middle-aged therapist, writer, teacher, mother, artist, and so on. Just as a deer, or a lion, or an anteater looks just like what it is, *I look like what I am*. More importantly, I look just like the person I set out to become.

I felt comforted to know that my outside matched my inside. I like who I am inside. Indeed, I have devoted my life to developing that person, making sure she got a good education and was both challenged and nurtured to become kind, compassionate, and generous. Who I am on the outside reflects quite precisely the priorities that have taken me into a life that feels full of purpose and connections. Realizing this was a tremendous relief. It helped me accept that I don't have to mount some heroic effort—including a severe diet and exercise regime—to change my appearance. I can move through the world just as I am.

What about *your* appearance, behaviors, and habits? Do you eat for some purpose other than to nourish yourself and perhaps share a meal with others? Do you eat to soothe yourself? Is your diet restrictive, because you are trying to reach or maintain a certain goal weight? Are you hungry and uncomfortable?

If you want to live without fear and quiet the impulse to criticize yourself, then you have to examine all the choices you make to see if they are driven by ugliphobia and the values promoted by the mainstream culture. As you evaluate each one, you might ask, "How does thinking this way affect my life? How would I feel if I let go of this concept? How would I feel if I decided that everyone—including me—is as beautiful as they need to be right now?"

Seriously, what would your life be like if you truly believed you were beautiful? Would you live differently? Would you have made different choices in the past if you had been certain you were beautiful? I have known many women who accepted marriage proposals because they believed they were too ugly to have many options. Their choices can seem tragic when you realize that their first mistake had been in accepting such a narrow definition of beauty that they fell outside the boundary.

If you consider people one by one, as distinct individuals, it's easier to find the beauty. With the exception of sociopaths, abusers, and those who are otherwise deranged, every human possesses the potential to be beautiful in spirit and intention. With the right attitude, we can see that beauty in the flicker of an eye or hear it in the lilting tone of a voice. It all depends on your perspective and your definitions. Naturalists can see beauty in a sea slug and hear it in the whine of a mosquito. (The slug's body is perfect for its purpose, and so is the mosquito's buzz.) To apply this perspective to human beings, consider someone like Stephen Hawking, the great scientist whose paralyzing physical disability gives him a contorted appearance. However, through his writing and lectures (he uses a computer to speak), Hawking demonstrates a breathtaking level of humanity and brilliance that make him quite appealing. When I see him on television he seems quite handsome to me, despite the fact that his physical self might be "ugly" according to the cultural definitions.

But you don't need genius or an extraordinary talent to claim your measure of beauty. Every person who pursues a life of generosity and shows empathy for others is beautiful to me. It's evident in a smile, a twinkling eye, or in the way the sunlight glints off of a stray hair. But here's the kicker: we're all ugly too.

In every person is all the ugliness that is part of the human condition. This shared reality is what wiser adults, who are brave, alert, and engaged, come to accept as they grow older. They understand that ugliness—as defined by the culture—is not a sign of failure but something to be expected, like illness and ultimately death. Life experience teaches us all this truth if we are open to it. It works something like this:

Every day we encounter flaws in others and in ourselves. Aging brings "ugliness" that is hard to deny, including flab, wrinkles, extra weight, drooping, and, well, you get the picture. If we have an open heart during these repeated encounters with so-called ugliness—including our own ugliness—we become less susceptible to feelings of disgust and more likely to accept ourselves and others. With disgust set to the side, we aren't moved to regard ourselves or others with contempt. Instead of being bigoted and rejecting, we can admire and connect with consistent kindness.

Consistency is essential. As the pioneering psychologist Gordon Allport noted in his classic book *The Nature of Prejudice*, sustained "friendly contact" is the best antidote for bigotry. This point is true whether you are dealing with racism or the bigotry of ugliphobia, which affects how we assess others and ourselves.

Be friendly to ourselves? Yes, because if you suffer from ugliphobia, then you may well be locked in a bigoted relationship with your own body. For example, for much of my life I believed that my body was inherently ugly or monstrous, and that although I struggled to control it, it would ultimately betray me. Some of these feelings and ideas were bestowed upon me by my mother, who was chronically ill and felt this way about herself. The rest were the product of growing up in a looks-obsessed culture. Once I understood these factors, and also understood what was wrong with the rules we all try to live by, I was able to reconsider my body with Allport's prescription in mind. I began, in a very deliberate way, to look for ways to appreciate my physical self. I developed gratitude for my body's service. It has taken me through more than five decades of life. I came to admire its creative energy, including the reproductive energy that gave me two children. With less effort than you might imagine, I was able to acknowledge all the pleasures and service my body provides. I could see that in some ways it meets the social standard for beauty and in other ways it is ugly.

My friends and family still get upset when I say I am ugly. They think that this statement is a sign that I've got "issues" and low self-esteem. When they talk to me about this book, they say that some readers and reviewers will criticize me for breaking the taboo and talking about ugliness so fully. I disagree. I think that it is liberating and empowering to take control of the U-word and the ugliness issue and define them for myself.

Getting comfortable with this concept—accepting that I am both ugly and beautiful, or attractive *and* unattractive—takes some work, but I have found tools that help. The first involves simply noticing that ugliphobia is rampant in our culture. If you pay attention you'll notice that casual and often critical references to someone's appearance will arise in personal conversations, e-mail exchanges, the marketplace, and media. With a more finely tuned personal radar you'll also notice that disgust and contempt are communicated with facial expressions and body language. In fact, we say far more to each other with nonverbal cues than words.

A sideways glance or a subtle shift in posture can signal disapproval that goes to the heart. Spend some time watching television or observing people in a park, and you'll notice the cues—both positive and negative—fly faster than words. Much of this communication involves what are called "microexpressions," which amount to barely perceptible twitches and movements. Microexpressions are so subtle that they usually don't register on a conscious level, but we feel their effects nevertheless. If you feel diminished or put down after an encounter with someone whose actual words weren't negative or demeaning, he may well have been flashing tiny signals of disapproval that flew beneath the radar to your heart and did some damage.

In the media, body language is most evident in still photos, which freeze the signals people send and allow us to study them at length. News and candid pictures often reveal contradictory feelings that a person is struggling to hide. Fear creeps around the eyes of a pop star who is supposed to be confident. A politician's supposedly loving spouse smiles at him, but stands at an angle that suggests she's really rejecting him. In advertising photos, which are constructed with great care and attention, models are coached, prodded, and directed to produce expressions that range from warm and seductive to icy cold and rejecting. The "glaring" displayed in many fashion and cosmetics ads, and which was recalled by an aspiring model in the earlier quote, is intentional. It communicates superiority and exclusivity. It is supposed to make you feel uncomfortable and insecure, as if the model possesses something better, which you must acquire to make the discomfort go away.

Glaring isn't the only negative expression you'll find in advertising. If you quickly thumb through the pages of a typical glossy magazine, the images strike you like it's a flip-book of rejection. You will see expressions of boredom, disdain, disgust, haughtiness, and knowing superiority all coated in flawless makeup and covered with the latest fashions. The effect on a reader is subtle and cumulative, but just as powerful as any words. In fact, in comparison, dealing with the statements made by bullies and others who put us down with attacks on our appearance is a fairly easy and uncomplicated matter.

If someone wants to point out that you have gray hair, flabby thighs, or a fat rear end (I have all three), it's simple enough to just agree. "Yes, I do have a fat ass," I'll say. "And you know, 65 percent of us are overweight, and diets fail about nine times out of ten." This kind of honesty will usually disarm a critic, but if the attack continues you can always add, "I try to be kind, even though I'm ugly. How about you?" This is somewhat aggressive—it puts the "hot potato of shame" back in their hands—but it also works.

When we recognize the effects of our ugliphobic environment, accept that we are all both ugly and beautiful as we are right now, and tell the truth about all of it, we naturally begin to look for ways to apply these insights in our own lives. With the right tools, and a willingness to do the work, this goal can be reached.

15

YOUR UGLY BIOGRAPHY

"Who's going to love you when your looks are gone?"

—Paul Simon

In an ideal world, it would be enough to recognize the false promises of the culture, identify the appearance-based bigotry that governs so much of our lives, and use truth-telling to recover from the effects. If this were possible we could move quickly from tyranny to liberation. Unfortunately, unless you were raised in extraordinary circumstances that made you strong and resistant to our bullying culture, it's not going to be that easy.

I believe that whether or not it rises to the level of an issue that would be recognized by all psychotherapists, the challenge we face in our bigoted culture traumatizes us and makes us genuinely phobic about our appearance. The evidence of trauma can be seen in the often detached, dissociated way we look at our faces and bodies, objectifying them in the same way they are objectified by the culture. Traumatized people withdraw—Have you ever hidden because of how you look?—and they tend to relive their traumatic moments in dreams or by anxiously going over events in their minds. Don't you recall, quite vividly, insults and moments of humiliation when you were made to feel ugly? I think these injuries do amount to trauma and that the pain lingers.

In pronounced cases, people who have been bullied and traumatized around the issue of appearance do develop more serious problems, including but not limited to eating disorders, body dysmorphic disorder, severe depression, and self-injuring behaviors like cutting and burning. But for the vast majority of us, the main psychological effects of growing up and living in an ugliphobic world run more toward chronic anxiety, discomfort about our own bodies, confusion when it comes to eating, insecurity, obsessing over our flaws, and acute self-consciousness.

I have experienced most of the ordinary symptoms of trauma and ugliphobia. Until I began to confront these issues more directly and learn how to think about them differently, I was plagued by the sense that my body was somehow separate from my self, that it was not under my own control, and would inevitably betray me. Like many people I could not be at all sure about what I saw in the mirror each day or whether I could ever trust any feedback I got about how I looked. A comment like "You look beautiful" would often prompt confusion and questions, instead of a sense that I was being appreciated. Because I knew that I was ugly I wondered about the "real" motivation of the person making the compliment: What did she want? Was it to manipulate me? Was it just a matter of being polite?

I have also been confused about food for much of my life. The origins of this trouble are partly cultural. Our entire society has a love/hate relationship with food because it provides pleasure but also threatens us with obesity. But most of us also have very specific and personal experiences with food that have affected our feelings and thinking more directly.

When I was growing up, the dinner table was a place of real tension where members of my family worked out many different hidden agendas. First there was the whole matter of preparing the meal. My mother, debilitated by Parkinson's disease, had so much trouble controlling her muscles that cooking was both a physical trial and an emotional challenge. I suspect now that she dreaded and resented it every day. Certainly I felt the stress mount in the hours before dinner. Then there was the value of the food itself and how it was apportioned. My father, the breadwinner, often complained about how much it cost to feed us and monitored who consumed what. (He got special treatment, always being served first.) One of my two older brothers, who was always hungry, ate so voraciously that I wondered if there would be anything left for me. The other brother joined my mother in keeping a close eye on my plate to make sure I wouldn't overeat. The language used by my family as they talked about eating—words like *gorge* and *glutton* were thrown about liberally—was so emotionally charged that I felt ashamed with every bite.

Sadly, many families pile extra emotional meaning onto the dinner table. This is all layered on top of the basic and natural human tendency to find comfort in eating. Food, especially fats and sugars, sends signals to pleasure centers in our brains. The chemical changes triggered by these signals can instantly make us feel calmer and happier. (This is why the faces of infants who are given a drop of sugar water flash with expressions of delight.) Combine the desire to be comforted by food with ambivalent and even punishing cultural attitudes about eating, and you get a stressed-out person who doesn't know how to feed herself.

As far back as I can recall, I have surveyed my plate at the beginning of every meal and thought, "It's not enough." My anxiety, which was high to begin with, rose as I ate. I couldn't tell if I was full or not, but I was nevertheless afraid that I wouldn't have enough. Over the years I became so disconnected from myself physically that I could no longer sense physical hunger and could only stop eating when the food was gone. As you might imagine, this problem caused a great deal of pain in my daily life, and I consider it one of the major challenges in my own effort to deal with the ugliness issue. It took me many years to realize what may be obvious: I didn't have enough, but it wasn't food that I was missing. It was the security and sense of self-worth that a properly nurtured child should feel.

Fortunately, understanding the story of my relationship with food has helped me manage it and my own ugliphobia. In fact it is a major element in the informal autobiography that I have worked on for many years in an effort to understand my experience in life and shape a happier, more grateful future.

What I call my "ugly biography" is a set of memories that I have assembled in a deliberate attempt to learn just how I acquired my attitudes about beauty, ugliness, and my own appearance. Some of my memories are your memories too, because they come from my contact with the mass media. Every kid who grew up with television learned that unattractive people generally suffer more and settle for less, while the beautiful ones reap rewards. Every once in a while a haughty beauty would get her comeuppance, but in general the programs and the advertising reinforced bigotry aimed at people who are supposedly unattractive. (According to the prevailing definition, this was nearly everyone who wasn't an actual media star.)

More important than these shared experiences are the personal encounters we had with real people whose words and actions taught us how to regard ourselves. How did your mother feel about her own appearance? How did your father feel about your mother's appearance? How did your parents react to your appearance? Did they compare you with your siblings, cousins, and friends? (My mother, who never had anything nice to say about my appearance, always called my friend Jill "stunning," which made me feel both ugly and jealous.) Were you ever given a score based on a one-to-ten scale? I bet you recall the number precisely.

In my therapy practice I have heard people talk about how they were practically tortured over their appearance when they were children. Among the actual nicknames I have heard people say they were given as kids are: pig, chub, toucan, beak, bird, Casper (for light skin), and pizza face. I have heard about mothers who talk to their daughters about which one of them is pretty and which one is not. I have also heard about fathers who have shamed their children so much that they have almost no self-regard at all.

Once you allow yourself to remember the words and acts that shaped your attitudes about your appearance, the memories come quickly. At first your recollections may be dominated by painful incidents from your past. It helps to acknowledge these incidents, affirm that they happened, and understand how they affect us. It also helps to know that the shame we felt in the moment and then carried ever since doesn't belong to us. Whenever someone is judged, discriminated against, or chastised for his appearance, the shame belongs to the aggressor, not the target.

Your biography, which I suggest you actually write down on paper, may include stories about your experience as a witness, when you saw someone else suffer because of prejudice or bullying. This is your experience of trauma by proxy, a true psychological injury. You also may recall times when you were the one calling names, rejecting others, and shaming them.

But while you cannot erase what you have done, you can understand the context and explore the influences that made you so aggressive. As we know, people who hurt others act, at least in part, because they have themselves been hurt. If this was true for you, then it was probably true for the people who made you the object of harsh words. Can you develop any empathy for the people who have been critical of you or yourself? Can you imagine why they said these things? Perhaps they had been tormented themselves (and continued to feel bad about their appearance) and were trying to be helpful to you. Many parents will put enormous pressure on their children in the hope that they can either spare them suffering or even help them win the advantages of beauty.

Beyond painful memories, I hope you also discover in your biography positive experiences including stories of people who saw you clearly and helped you feel valued. Some of us were raised in families where appearance didn't matter as much as character, and we learned healthy lessons about our bodies. Most of us encountered at least some friends and teachers and other adults who treated us with respect and made us feel accepted. In these moments we received input that offered support for changing both our feelings and our behaviors.

Your biography will reveal the origins of many of your thoughts, feelings, and behaviors. Can you see how your experience with ugliness has affected your life? Has it influenced you to be more or less adventurous? Has it made you bold or shy? Did it play a role in your decision to apply for a certain job or scholarship? Does it influence the way you talk to yourself, about yourself, as you go through each day? Has it led you to justify using unkind words about yourself and others?

We all internalize the messages delivered to us by the outside world, especially those that come from the people around us when we are young. A good example of this process can be seen in the whole issue of reproduction. As they mature, girls and women hear that their value depends on being attractive so that they can get married and one day have children. Those who do not fulfill this cultural notion, either by choice or by circumstances beyond their control, often wind up feeling ugly because they haven't had children. (The words used to describe them—*barren, childless, spinster*—have obvious negative connotations.) Since millions of wonderful women lead beautiful lives without children, the bias here is obvious and unfair. Nevertheless, it must be recognized and confronted because it often contributes to feelings of self-doubt and a pattern of self-criticism.

If you worry and bully yourself over your appearance you are undoubtedly channeling voices from the past and the bigotry of our culture. If, for example, you never seem able to eat a meal without performing some sort of emotional gymnastics, then, like me, your experience with ugliness has shaped when you eat, what you eat, how much you eat, and why you eat.

For those who are especially strict about their diet, controlling food is likely to be a way to compensate for feeling out of control in other parts of life. By restricting what we eat, measuring and tabulating, we can give ourselves the idea that we are doing something about our ugliness. But even as we do this, we're actually handing control of our identities over to a tyrannical and impossible-to-satisfy culture. We may feel momentarily successful when we spend an entire day hungry, but if we have also felt edgy, distracted, depressed, or low-energy, then we haven't really been in control. Better to go back to the very first assumption we make: that "control" is the ideal. This belief suggests that something awful would happen if we simply relaxed. In fact, nothing bad will happen if we are simply ourselves. Indeed, we might even discover that when we stop making such a big deal out of eating, its ceases to be such a powerful issue.

The same truth applies when we focus inordinately on how we dress or use accessories and makeup. An obsession with these issues may have been born in the accumulation of painful experiences. Now it could serve as a distraction from other important issues. It's very easy, when we are unsettled, to make something external, like our clothes, the focus, and to work very hard to feel better by getting the perfect "look." This doesn't work when the thing that is actually troubling us is on the inside, not the outside.

Fortunately, the biography practice can open our minds to the inter-play of past experience, current feelings, and our ongoing behavior. If you let it, it can help you recognize when encounters with other people, the media, or even stray thoughts about your appearance make you anxious, sad, or otherwise distressed. These events can be considered "triggers" for deep-seated memories of trauma. Once triggered, the memories can produce powerful feelings that don't seem to match our real-life circum-stances. Incidents that might otherwise roll off your back instead make you feel truly frightened, angry, or even panicked, as if you were under attack. (When this happens something has triggered the so-called "fight-or-flight" instinct and sent a surge of cortisol through your body. As mentioned earlier, chronic high levels of cortisol have debilitating effects on your body, contributing to weight gain, heart disease, bone loss, and other problems.)

If an offhand comment about your outfit makes you tense up all over and starts your heart pounding with anxiety, you are having an emo-tional "flashback" to a time when you were hurt very deeply. Though not as acute, these episodes are not unlike the flashbacks experienced by victims of profound trauma due to violence. Flashbacks alter your experience of reality, and the pain that they cause sends us running for relief.

When we don't recognize what is happening and just experience the pain, we run the risk of seeking relief in less productive and even destruc-tive ways. Lots of people shop, eat, or use drugs or alcohol to cope with the uneasiness or hurt provoked by a flashback. I call this the Band-Aid-on-a-bullet-wound approach, and if this is your tendency, then you know that it doesn't work for long. The little buzz or quiet relief you get is quickly followed by confusion or perhaps remorse as you notice the empty ice cream bowl or the total on your credit card statement. As the pain returns, it's easy to fall into the trap of self-condemnation. We scold ourselves and, literally, repeat the abuse that traumatized us in the first place.

A therapist can be very helpful if we get stuck in the cycle of trauma and flashback.

You can also begin to cope with flashbacks in a positive way—by writing in a journal, reaching out to a friend, or talking to yourself in comforting terms. If you notice that you are falling into the habit of self-criticism, don't use this realization to further judge and condemn yourself. Just begin taking note of it. Try writing down the time, place, and message you send to yourself. Look for patterns that can be interrupted and assumptions you might change. Many of the judgments we make about ourselves are based on choices, not universal truths.

I'm especially struck by how our choice of words—even the ones that are part of the "inner dialogue" we have with ourselves—can reveal the depth of our pain. When I hear someone say "I feel ugly" or "I feel fat," I know that what she is really saying is that she feels insecure, depressed, angry, or some other powerful emotion. "Fat" is not a feeling. Neither is "ugly." The fact that we use these words to describe how we feel proves the power of appearance to define everything about us, including what's in our hearts. Typically these expressions are followed by self-recrimination and self-punishment. ("I feel so ugly because I ate like a pig last night.") This sets up a cycle of negative self-talk that never leads to anything good. However, it is an extremely common way of thinking, as you'll see in the "Speak Out" appendix at the end of this book.

It would be difficult for anyone to simply break the habit of self-criticism, but it is possible to limit this way of thinking. The first thing you can do is try to change your vocabulary. Since "ugly" and "fat" aren't true emotions, every time you are about to use these words to describe a feeling, stop and think about the genuine emotion behind them. If, for example, you are actually feeling insecure, then let yourself feel insecure.

Then consider responding with a little reflection on all your positive traits. When do you feel proud of yourself? Not pretty, not numb, but proud? Focus on those experiences and do whatever you can to repeat them.

Now, I know that this positive thinking has limited power. (My apologies to Norman Vincent Peale.) Ugliphobia and the habit of self-criticism will not be stilled in a moment, no matter how much willpower you apply. However, it is possible to limit the effect. One way to do this would be to schedule some daily "ugly time." Take a half hour or so and let your mind wander through the hall of shame. Pick on your clothes, your skin, and your hair all you want. But when the half-hour is finished, try to accept that those thoughts have been quarantined for the day. Then give yourself permission to enjoy the other twenty-three and a half hours in the day free of all this self-hatred.

Trauma recovery requires time, safety, and affirmation. (By affirmation I mean that we must trust in our own experience, believe our own reality). This is all the more true when it comes to our experience with a culture that is obsessed with appearance and constantly assaults us with bigoted judgments. If we aren't being graded and insulted personally, then we get to be traumatized by proxy as we see the famous and not-so-famous subjected to mockery and derision on screen and in print. How do we recover and get strong when there are constant occasions of re-injury? The answer is the same for everyone. You need to believe in your own experiences and story.

To aid this process you might consider reducing the number of times per day or week that you consult a mirror or the bathroom scale to check on your appearance or weight. Mirrors and scales allow us to step outside of our internal experience to "prove factually" that we are ugly or fat. Often, I'll be feeling perfectly happy until I pass a mirror or other reflective surface and the "truth" shocks and horrifies me. My good mood can turn into self-loathing, and I feel ashamed of having felt good before I saw the "truth" in the mirror. The same happens with the scale. As an antidote to this problem, I recommend a kind of diet, similar to the media diets some people use to limit their daily intake of information via the media so they don't feel overloaded. When you reduce your use of the mirror and the scale, you give yourself more time to simply be yourself.

Biography, emotional redefinitions, the mirror/scale diet, and quarantine from self-criticism can bring us a better perspective. They all belong in the toolbox of techniques we can use to confront the ugly problem, change our perspective, and begin defining ourselves according to our own values. They are based on some of the essential methods used in psychotherapy by people who are overcoming trauma and phobias. Phobias can be especially difficult to work with, but our toolbox does offer a little more help. One is the practice of desensitization. The other involves a direct challenge to the substance of your phobia.

First, a word about desensitization. We all know that people with phobias related to flying or insects or elevators, for example, sometimes find relief through gradual exposure to the object of their fear. With the help of a therapist or coach, a few minutes with a spider is followed by a few minutes more until eventually you are able to sit calmly as the spider crawls up your arm.

With ugliphobia, desensitization might begin with a bit of meditation on the possibility that something about you really is imperfect. Maybe your eyes are not equidistant from the bridge of your nose or one earlobe dangles lower than the other. Maybe, just maybe, your figure isn't perfect or the number on the bathroom scale isn't what you want. (I know that I could use the current media template for beauty and find something "wrong" with every inch of my body.)

Ask yourself what it would mean if one or two of your so-called "beauty problems" were real. Would your life suddenly fall apart if you were a little bit ugly? What would you lose if you stopped worrying about the extra pounds, or that dangling earlobe? Can you try allowing yourself to just be ugly for a short period of time? Could you put on rumpled, mismatched clothes and let the neighbors see you? Can you look at yourself in the mirror on a day when you don't look your "best" and still smile with warmth and love?

You may resist experimenting with ugliness, but in reality, we are all living with our ugliness every day. Everyone else *already sees* our ugly bits and has decided to either accept us or not with those parts included. Nothing could possibly change if we recognize them ourselves, except our own feelings. If we are able to gaze at our own imperfections with kindness and affection, just as our friends do, then we might begin to make peace with them. If instead of hating the bunions on your feet you decide they are simply part of a person who has walked more than a few miles in life, you might appreciate the fact that you have made it this far in life and be happy about what you have experienced and learned along the way.

As you consider yourself with a kinder perspective you might also imagine that some of the "parts" you hate are actually admired and prized by others. That nose you think is too big is noble in someone's eyes. The softer flesh that you work so hard to make disappear may be just the thing that draws your partner near. Your admirers, it turns out, don't view you with the stereotypes that lead to bigotry and rejection. Their hearts and minds are more open and less controlled than you fear. And the ones who really love you see you in your entirety, as a whole and unique person.

A deeper understanding of this kind of acceptance can be gained from making an inventory of the people you love and admire who may not find their way onto one of *People* magazine's "sexiest" or "most beautiful" lists. For example, among the people I happen to love is a smallish, baldish, middle-aged man who has more belly than he really needs. (I find all of these "flaws" loveable.) I admire a long list of teachers, students, patients, friends, and colleagues. If you met them you might notice all sorts of imperfections, but somehow they don't register in my mind.

We can look past the so-called ugliness of people, even things that are supposedly disgusting, whenever we are able to view them with love and acceptance. If you have ever seen someone through a terrible illness, you know what I am talking about. When the body loses its ability to function, when it leaks and decays right before our eyes, it can produce awful sights and sounds and smells. And yet we stay close as someone we love suffers. We don't turn away. In the process we learn to accept everything that's usually covered up and hidden out of fear. This is why hospitals and hospices can be places of intensely positive human experience. In crisis and as death approaches we can drop all the artifice that we use to protect ourselves from "ugly." Forced to be defenseless, people show their true nature, and it is almost always something good.

Almost any kind of raw and unsanitized experience can deliver us from the numbed and superficial existence that we think protects us and into the real world where there's nothing wrong with messiness and imperfection. This truth came into clear focus for me after the 9/11 tragedy in New York City. For days and weeks the relatives and friends carried photos of people who were missing from place to place, showing them in hopes of finding a clue to their whereabouts. The pictures showed people in their natural, unpolished state, and few if any could have been mistaken for fashion models or pop stars. And yet the love shown by the surviving friends and relatives made each missing person seem truly valued and therefore beautiful.

Most of us know people, and perhaps other beings, who matter to us in a way that transcends appearances. If you want to feel inspired, make your own list of people you love and admire, and next to their names make a note about the qualities—courage, kindness, creativity, and so on—that attract you to them. Then make a list of the traits they have that society would call ugly. Include people in your life and famous people you might look up to. (Mother Theresa? Eleanor Roosevelt?) When you're finished, add your own name and characteristics, not to the bottom of the list, but to the top. It's where you belong, with all of your thoroughly human and completely acceptable qualities. Good, bad, beautiful, ugly—it's all in each one of us.

16

SELF-CARE

"*It is better to look good than to feel good.*"

—"Fernando," as played by
Billy Crystal on Saturday Night Live

Fernando's words of wisdom—placing appearance above all other
human values—became a catchphrase that the character repeated often
on the program *Saturday Night Live* in the mid-1980s. We laughed
because Billy Crystal's parody of a preening movie star was extreme, but
also because it rang true. In Hollywood it seemed like formulaic good
looks were the keys to success, and to stay in the game you needed to
look the part. Fernando's taut and tanned skin and brilliant teeth—"my
American smile"—were such obvious signs of desperate artifice they
were laughable. (At least on TV.)

But then a strange, if not funny, thing happened. The cosmetic interventions that would make an aging star like Fernando seem so extreme
gradually became mainstream.

Public demand for caps, tooth veneers, and dental bleaching exploded.
(During one five-year period, the amount Americans spent on tooth
bleaching tripled.) Tanning salons sprouted in shopping malls, and a host
of new products—Botox, crease-fillers, creams, and lotions—were invented

to help get skin that looked like a movie star's. Gradually, the standard for all of us came to match what we saw in the media. If you wanted to look good you had to have gleaming teeth and smooth skin, and you needed to devote the necessary time and money to have both. Similar standards evolved for the rest of the body and the pursuit of these elusive goals became a matter of "self-care."

Today, "taking care of yourself" is widely interpreted to mean "pampering" your outsides in order to prevent or eliminate anything "ugly." To achieve this goal, most women follow certain regimes—morning, evening, weekly, monthly—that consume hours of their time and a good portion of their incomes. My own routines include skin care in the morning and evening, and periodic exfoliation. I also devote time to shaving, bathing, styling my hair, and applying makeup. In the summer when I wear sandals and flip-flops, I adopt an extra weekly ritual involving scrubs, pumice, cuticle cutting, and nail polish to reduce the evidence that my feet are as old and tired as they are. Sometimes this process feels good. I like having soft, clean skin on my feet. But there are other times when I suspect that I'm practicing this ritual—and others—out of fear.

I often experience the fear of ugliness and rejection when applying makeup, getting my hair styled, or doing any of a dozen other "self-care" exercises. It seems strange to scrub or cut or shave or primp out of fear, because nothing we do out of fear could possibly feel good or be defined as "caring." Once you realize this, you start to suspect that a great many of the things we are supposed to do in order to take care of ourselves actually have the opposite effect.

If these self-care options are not chosen freely, if we feel pressured and bullied and act compulsively, then on some deep level we're going to experience them as forced and even as a betrayal of our true selves. The truth is that the so-called beauty strategies and indulgences sold to us in the media are not right for everyone. But we adopt them nevertheless, compromising our time and our financial resources as we seek safety in the notion that we must do whatever we can to avoid ugliness.

The compromises aren't too difficult when you are young and strong and they are limited in number. Young faces don't need expensive firming treatments and young feet can handle high fashion shoes. But as you age you have to add more "self-care" to your life. Most of us do this automatically, simply adopting whatever practice we're supposed to use to stave off age and ugliness. Without much thought we take up the battle against what one advertiser calls "the visible signs of aging," arming ourselves with strategies and products.

Gradually the effort begins to make serious demands on your time and your wallet. You may begin to wonder just how much artifice you are going to practice in order to meet someone else's idea of what might make us attractive. Finally, as you notice that life holds many better ways to spend your time and think about yourself, you start to consider making active choices about what constitutes "self-care." This reconsideration begins with making your own definition of "self" and your own definition of "care."

As you seek to define yourself as a person, search your character and personality to find the qualities that have nothing to do with appearance. Based merely on the fact that you have opened this book and come this far with me, I would bet that you are a bright, curious person who is interested in ideas and brave about exploring them. I would also wager that if you look closely you'll find admirable traits like empathy, generosity, and creativity, as well as a unique combination of skills and talents.

Some of the qualities you'll notice in yourself are the product of your basic temperament and genetic makeup. Others come from the outside, and have been developed over time and through experience. These traits represent the positive influence of other people and the larger culture. I am grateful that along with its ugliphobia and the pressure to conform, society also offers us teachers and traditions that can help us to feel more comfortable and accepting of ourselves. One of my favorites is the Japanese notion of wabi-sabi, which holds that imperfection and impermanence are the essence of nature and can define what is actually beautiful.

Buddhist in origin, wabi-sabi thought emerged in Japan about eight hundred years ago. Roughly translated, the word *wabi* refers to rustic nature and *sabi* connotes the beauty that comes with aging. Everything in the world, including people, the elements of nature, and manmade objects can be considered wabi-sabi. In objects, wabi-sabi can be seen in the patina that might develop on the surface of a piece of metal or wood or the stitches that have been used to repair a piece of cloth. The wear and tear are signs of usefulness and accumulated experiences. They make the objects, like people, unique, and through their history, some-thing to appreciate.

The signs of wabi-sabi on my body include every wrinkle, sagging bit of flesh, and scar. Especially the scars. The one on my back is left from an emergency operation that saved me from paralysis. My belly carries the evidence of gall bladder surgery that ended weeks of terrible pain and the scar from a hysterectomy that marked a turning point in my life. The line under my chin, left from my plastic surgery, reminds me of the experi-ence I had with my first book and the struggle that led me to a deeper understanding of the ugliness issue. Every imperfection on my body, whether it recalls the passage of time or a moment of crisis and decision, represents the progress of my life and the process that made me ever-more myself.

It seems a simple thing to accept that everything changes, that perfec-tion is impossible, and aging is inevitable. But compare this idea to the values promoted by the Greeks. Their ideal was represented by marble statues of youths with perfectly toned and proportioned bodies. Something in human nature led the Greeks to dream that this perfection was possible and to pursue it. In contrast, the symbol of wabi-sabi is a handmade tea bowl with an irregular shape and imperfect glazing.

Wabi-sabi requires you to accept that imperfection—in objects, yourself, and everyone around you—is the essence of life. The challenge in wabi-sabi is in seeing clearly, appreciating what you see, and letting go of illusions. Among the illusions worth abandoning, in my view, are:

Beauty and sexiness are synonymous.

Some people are ugly by definition while others are not.

Beauty is a one-size-fits-all commodity.

Youth is the essence of beauty.

Aging brings ugliness that must be delayed by all means possible.

Imagine replacing these illusions with matching wabi-sabi insights. You would then realize that everyone is at all times ugly *and* beautiful. The change and decay that come with the passage of time is the one thing that connects us with certainty to the entire universe. Liberated by wabi-sabi, we don't have to fear imperfection or impermanence because they define our existence. Knowing this, it's possible to then define how you "care" for yourself in your own terms. You can care for your body, mind, and soul by nourishing them and providing them with rest and stimulation. You can care for your life by establishing and cultivating relationships, creative outlets, meaningful work—the choices are all yours.

The choices include how you care for your appearance. If you enjoy every single thing you do to keep your skin, hair, nails, body, and so on in a certain condition, there is no reason to stop any of them. But if you haven't made an affirmative choice in favor of these various rituals, give yourself a chance to review them. Challenged this way, most of us discover we can let something go, but doing this will require a little courage.

A case in point, for me, was my commitment to dyeing my hair, which began long before I had any gray hairs at all. Hair dyeing is one of those things that women seem to embrace as a necessity, especially as we age. Worried that we may be losing the shiny luster that suggests fertility and health—and therefore beauty—we turn to products that promise it and more. Look at the boxes on the drugstore shelf and you see women who look as nearly perfect as possible, with incredibly thick, silky, evenly colored hair. L'Oreal says "You're worth it," and Clairol promises to make you "healthy looking." At the Garnier website you learn that:

> Garnier appeals to the type of woman who is self-confident yet seeks to improve her appearance. By taking care of herself she reveals her inner beauty and other people are drawn to her. For Garnier the aim of beauty is to feel happy and at ease with others. It's about taking care.

There's that concept again—taking care. This infers that dyeing your hair is a matter of your genuine well-being, like eating properly and getting medical check-ups. Conversely, not dyeing your hair would mean that you are not taking care of yourself. You are not trying to reveal your inner beauty, draw people to you, or feel happy and at ease. You are, instead, a slacker who doesn't care and isn't taking care.

The trouble with this argument is two-fold. First, nobody would consider hair dye an essential part of self-care without this kind of advertising. The second is that the products generally don't work. While expensive custom dye jobs done at salons can sometimes turn out well, I have never seen anyone get the hair they see on the box from the product that is *inside* the box. It may happen, somewhere in the universe, but it has never happened to me or anyone I know. (I can't count the number of hair color traumas that have been discussed in my psychotherapy practice.) We get, if we're lucky, fairly consistent color that covers gray hair but doesn't really match anything in nature. Of course, everyone is so accustomed to seeing dyed hair that we no longer expect to see natural color. The plum reds, two-tone blonds, and other artificial tints delivered by chemical dyes don't seem unusual because they are not. Millions of women adopt these colors and wear them for years. I did it for fifteen years.

Why do we pursue these habits? Because as with so many other self-care rituals, once you start dyeing your hair it becomes difficult to stop.

If it's a so-called permanent dye, you have to wait for it to grow out, which can mean having two or even three-color hair (counting gray) for months. If it's not permanent dye then you have to endure a shorter transition, but you still have to put up with looking "bad" while the color fades and your true color emerges.

Women talk about their hair color almost as much as they talk about their weight and diet. It's such a serious subject that when writer Anne Kreamer published a book about her decision to forego coloring—it was called *Going Gray*—she sparked a debate that raged for months in national magazines and on TV talk shows. Kreamer challenged the idea that older women can't be beautiful and even attractive with their real hair. The book came out in 2007 and became one of two inspirations for my own flight from the tyranny of hair coloring. The other was a mouse.

It all started when our cats chased a tiny field mouse under the radiator in the den. (It was late autumn and like crickets and other creatures, the mouse was looking for a nice warm place to spend the winter.) My husband grabbed some salad tongs and removed the tiny worried creature. He put it into a box, and released it in the woods, but not before I admired its bright eyes and shiny coat.

For all of my life, I had been told that my mother had "mousy-brown" hair and I thought I needed to dye mine to avoid the same dreaded mousiness. But here was an actual mouse, with real mousy-brown hair, and it was perfectly fine. Actually, it was soft, lustrous, and I much preferred it to the high maintenance "lightest golden brown" I had been using. I thought, "If that's what mousy brown looks like, sign me up!"

As you might imagine, my hairdresser disagreed. In fact she was so set against me abandoning hair color that it ended our relationship, which until this point had lasted more than twenty years. I found one who understood me and what I wanted. He cut my hair short and encouraged me to stop coloring cold turkey—no touchups, no highlights, nothing.

I thought I would need great strength to follow through. In fact, I did not. Instead, when the first gray hairs came in, I noticed that they sparkled in my bathroom mirror like tinsel. Based on my own standards, I loved it. As the years have passed I have noticed that the hair color I sported in old photos looks like it belongs on someone else's head. In the years since my fateful decision I have spared myself dozens of dyeing sessions and put all that time and money to better use. (I also don't miss the "evidence" of my dyeing sessions, which used to leave my shower tile looking like the blood-spattered motel bathroom in the movie *Psycho*.)

For me, hair color was just the beginning. As I entered my fifties I accepted that I was never going to look twenty-five again, and that life was too short to pour as much time and energy as I had into this impossible pursuit. I had other priorities. I've also come to realize that this is a deeply ethical issue. If I love myself, then I have an obligation to be as healthy and happy as I can be.

Of course you don't have to be middle-aged to adopt a more empathetic and accepting attitude toward yourself. Self-criticism is harmful at any age. Good nutrition, a bit of exercise, and proper rest are essential whether you are ten years old or a hundred. The same is true for creative outlets and relationships that give us support. Age is not a factor when it comes to accepting all the positive inputs that life has to offer. When we nurture ourselves and others with the deliberate intention of fostering growth and happiness, we are putting love into action. No one deserves this kind of "care" more than you do, and no one is better able to provide it than you. This is the essence of self-care.

17

EMBRACING MEDUSA

"Character cannot be developed in ease and quiet.
Only through experience of trial and suffering can the soul be
strengthened, ambition inspired, and success achieved."

—HELEN KELLER

Whether it's the ancient wisdom of wabi-sabi, the modern common sense in Anne Kreamer's *Going Gray*, or the simple example of a tiny field mouse, we can find inspiration for an alternative to ugliphobia expressed in many different ways. However, the message is the same: When we reject our differences and the changes that come to us all with time—labeling them ugly and repulsive—we are really rejecting ourselves and the essential reality of nature.

Nothing in nature is perfect, and every living thing ages, decays, and dies. If we deny this truth or try to defy it, the struggle will take up so much time and energy we'll miss out on much of what we might enjoy in life. If we can learn to accept it and not fear it, we can make the most of the gift that is our time here on Earth.

The solution to ugliphobia is not a generic prescription. We must each find for ourselves the right mix of attitudes and values to fit our circumstances, hopes, and dreams. However, I think we must all start the pursuit by letting ourselves off the hook. Before I devised the philosophies and strategies for fighting my own fears of ugliness, I assumed the problem was me. Whenever my clothes, makeup, shoes, or accessories didn't look as they looked on the mannequin or in the magazines, I concluded that I must be so ugly that the stuff that works for everyone else simply won't work on me. If everyone else looked pretty in spring pastels except me, then I must be the problem.

The sense of failure drove me to make an even more furious effort to conform, which only led to more failure. All this happened because I had let the culture and other people define ugliness for me and then terrify me into thinking that to be ugly would be the worst fate imaginable. This is precisely what the Greeks did to Medusa. They took a figure who was a symbol of the positive power of all women and redefined her as ugly. Then they made her ugliness into something lethal.

At this point in the journey that is this book, you might expect me to urge you to embrace all that is represented by the frightening Medusa, with her snake hair and fangs and claws and power. Well, I do think we need to accept and incorporate the Ugly Medusa's characteristics into our self-concept, because her ugliness (I'd simply call it human-ness) is inside every one of us. Medusa wasn't a monster. She was a woman who had been raped, blamed for the crime, and then turned into a nightmarish figure. If she raged at the world before she was killed, I think she had the right. Anyone treated the way she was treated would be angry and likely to lash out.

It's not enough, however, to accept the aspects of Medusa that symbolize the struggle against injustice and the protest against being defined by others. We also need to embrace the original, pre-Greek Medusa as well. She's the one who made grain, fruit, and vegetables grow out of the earth and blessed all living things. The original Medusa was not frightening, but life-giving, and without her gifts the ancients could not survive. If today we can accept and hold inside us *both* versions of Medusa, we might actually strike a blow against ugliphobia and make our culture and society much more humane and our own lives much more peaceful and purposeful.

When we accept and empathize with both versions of Medusa—allowing ourselves to see that she represents the complete human experience—it becomes much easier to take responsibility for our thoughts, feelings, and behaviors and to change what we want to change. After all, we alone are responsible for our choices to be cruel to ourselves or others. Once you know the truth, your upbringing, culture, and other influences cannot be considered excuses or justifications for continuing to be part of the ugly problem. And once you know better, you alone are responsible for accepting yourself and others. This involves three key steps:

- Stop pretending that you have nothing to do with what our culture defines as ugly. As social animals we cannot survive apart from our culture, but as we depend on it, we also absorb its values and transmit them, for good or bad, to others.
- Accept that all the crookedness, decay, mess, and foul odor that might ever be part of the human condition *is* part of you. There is nothing inherently bad or evil about this truth, especially when you also admit that everything that is admirable, generous, kind, and creative *is also* inside of you.
- Acknowledge that the power to decide how you express your human-ness is yours. And as you make these choices you are creating—I'd use the word *fashioning*—your self.

When we make truly conscious choices about our values, beliefs, and priorities we give ourselves permission to draw from all that is possible. This isn't to say that you can simply choose to be a great artist or athlete or scientist. Our achievements and creations depend on variations in talents, intelligences, and circumstances. However, you can choose to challenge the appearance-based bigotry that dominates our culture. You can choose to express your own sense of beauty and to respect how others express themselves. You can choose to live openly and without fear, and you can choose to welcome others to do the same.

Each of these shifts in attitude and action—taking responsibility, making choices, and opening ourselves to others—represents a challenge that will provoke crosscurrents of emotions. Consider first the issue of responsibility. I cannot imagine how anyone could be born into our world and avoid participating in anti-ugly bigotry. As children, adolescents, and young adults we are most receptive to all the messages issued by our parents, siblings, social circle, and the larger culture. If you are constantly bombarded with certain definitions of ugliness and beauty, and trained to associate one with loss and another with gain, you have a tendency to adopt these prejudices for yourself.

The pernicious and all-encompassing quality of ugliphobia means that most of us have rejected, taunted, shamed, or demeaned someone because of his appearance. Very few girls go through school without being both the victim of shunning and a perpetrator. Very few boys escape being rejected for the way they look or reach adulthood without having heaped scorn on some "ugly" girl or "disgusting" boy. To avoid painful emotions we tend to bury these experiences and try to move on. But once you awaken to certain ugly truths—say, by reading this book— the memories tend to return along with feelings of isolation, alienation, anger, and shame, just to name a few.

It's comparatively easy to accept and "own" the times when we were hurt by others. However, as anyone who ever behaved like a bully will attest, it's difficult to accept the truth about your own aggression. During my work on this book I have heard from several women who confessed to me that they had been bigots of the type made famous by the book *Queen Bees and Wannabees* and the related movie *Mean Girls* (2004).

Each one recalled with some shame the way she had used words and social strategies to hurt girls and boys they thought were ugly. Mean girls and boys freeze ugly classmates and neighbors out of groups, they spread lies about them, and even taunt their victims openly while inviting others to join in.

One woman who talked to me in therapy about her experience as an adolescent who tormented other ugly girls felt profoundly guilty about what she had done. In therapy Terry gradually realized that she had felt extreme pressure to conform and feared that she might never live up to the expectations of her family, which she had internalized. By turning on others she had relieved some of her own torment, replacing it with a temporary sense of power and safety. As an adult she felt ashamed of the bigotry she had expressed but understood that it hadn't started with her. She also saw that as she had matured out of the "mean girl" posture, the only person she had continued to torment was herself.

Long after Terry had learned it was unfair to judge others by their appearance, she still clung to the belief that she had to always look perfect. The "look" she pursued included all of the external signs of beauty and success, including the best fashion, hair color, body, education, career, and home she could attain. She had worked overtime to get these outward signifiers of superiority and goodness, and believed that the disciplined, dogged pursuit of these things was a sign of her high character. This kind of approach reminds me of the coach who drives his team through the most grueling workouts, telling them that the pursuit of victory will make them people of character, but then allows them to use dirty tricks in the game. The coach may be making his players into winners on the field but he's not building character traits that will make them happy in life. Terry may have been driving herself to be perfect, but she was also setting herself up to be terribly unhappy.

When she realized how much time and effort she put into her exterior, and how little she devoted to her inner self, Terry saw that because of her own ugliphobia she was still treating herself like a mean girl. For a while this realization made her angry with herself because she believed she should have been strong enough to control every one of her own attitudes and behavior.

It helped Terry to study the landmark experiments on social influence on behavior, including Milgram's electric shock experiment and Zimbardo's Stanford prison project. When Zimbardo finished his work he was struck by the enormous influence of the little society he had created. When it came to human behavior, he noted, culture and social pressure were far more powerful than "personality traits, character, [or] will power." In light of Zimbardo's findings, Terry may have been responsible for how she treated others and herself, but she had also been under the influence of extremely powerful forces that few people can even recognize.

Fortunately, addressing ugliphobia doesn't require we make immediate and sweeping changes in our lives. It only requires adopting a conscious, active approach to our lives. Terry genuinely enjoyed much of what she was doing, especially her job and her relationship with her partner. But as she fashioned herself with a more deliberate purpose she decided to make friends with the forty-year-old face and body she saw in the mirror every day and cut back on the time and energy she poured into altering its appearance. She allowed herself more moments when she chose comfort over conformity—ditching spiked heels in favor of flats and choosing not to squeeze herself into Spanx every day. She let some new, daring colors into her wardrobe and even went to work in something other than a business suit.

Some of the energy and time Terry saved with these changes was diverted to interests she had long harbored but rarely explored, including art, travel, and writing. The rest she invested in her relationships, where she tried to be more relaxed and open about who she was. Like many women, Terry was shocked to discover the man she lived with actually loved her less-than-perfect parts and didn't even notice whether she wore makeup at breakfast.

As Terry's experience with her partner showed, the antidote for shame is honest, safe connection to others, not unthinking conformity. And one of the great wonders of genuine relationships is that they can grow stronger when we reveal ourselves in all of our complexity, including the bits that make us feel insecure. This opening-up takes courage because we all fear being rejected by anyone who sees us clearly. This will happen sometimes, because the last remaining acceptable form of bigotry—anti-ugliness—remains powerful and few people recognize its impact. If you accept yourself first, and know that you may get rejected from time to time, the negative experiences don't hurt as much as you expect. And the positive ones will bring you to a new level of understanding and closeness that will make the risk worth it. Admitting one's ugliness is a liberating and exciting breakthrough. It affirms that ugliness is not a failure, but simply an expected part of the human condition, and nothing to be feared.

As I was writing this book I saw a remarkable confirmation of this concept—that owning our ugliness is liberating—during a meal with some new friends. A devoted couple who were obviously open and accepting with each other, Allan and Georgia are brilliant, creative, and perhaps the least pretentious people I have ever met. Before we had finished our first course we were telling war stories from our pasts, including some remarkably painful tales that anyone eavesdropping might find horrifying.

We laughed as we played a game of "Can You Top This?" in which life experiences that would surely qualify as humiliating, embarrassing, or even "ugly" according to the standard definition, became simple examples of how hard it can be to find your way in a world full of prejudice, double messages, and inhumane standards. The stories included, literally, tales of childhood abuse, sexual disasters, loss, grief, and shame. But with each shy and then boisterous revelation of an injury or indignity, we laughed harder and felt closer as the confessions demonstrated how much we shared and how eagerly we wanted to be honest and whole.

As each confession was met with acceptance, our smiles and laughter honored the absurdity of life. It's a great relief to own all of our experiences, share them, and be accepted. At no other time will you feel safer and more loved. And how you look has nothing to do with it.

EPILOGUE: PASS IT ON

"When spider webs unite, they can tie up a lion."

—Ethiopian Proverb

The truth about ugliphobia can be overwhelming. It is biological in origins but largely a social construct, and it affects every imaginable aspect of our lives including our physical and mental health, relationships, education, work, art, religious expression, sexuality, and self-concept. Sometimes when you realize the extent of bigotry that surrounds you, and that it can inhabit your own mind, it seems impossible to stand against it.

Fortunately, social influence can work its magic in a positive way, too. Each one of us who awakens to the influence of institutions, media, the marketplace, and our own words can begin to change not just ourselves but the social environment. After all, we are participants in our culture and can, in ways big and small, change it.

Some change is already underway. Throughout the industrialized world, writers, parents, teachers, and others have begun to speak against the influence of extreme media images, like pictures of emaciated models with artificially inflated breasts. In Spain and Italy public officials are actually monitoring the health of models. The French National Assembly has considered a ban on pro-anorexia websites, and in Great Britain, Parliament is considering a law to require that retouched and Photoshopped images be labeled as such.

Rules and regulations can be a clumsy way to change social attitudes, especially when they bump up against competing ideals like freedom of the press and the value of artistic expression. This is why it's encouraging to see that change is also occurring as a matter of self-interest, as some leaders in business recognize the longer-term value of connecting with people on a more humane level. Since 2004, Unilever, the giant consumer product company, has famously pursued a "real beauty" advertising campaign that foregoes the usual young-super-tall-and-skinny-models and features instead images of women of all different ages, sizes, and shapes. Advertisements for the company's Dove products talk about how modern society has a "distorted" sense of beauty and display some of the tricks used to make models look "super." Instead of presenting supposedly perfect-looking women, Dove ads show more ordinary women who seem happy about who they are and how they look. The ads associate Dove products with a sense of acceptance and respect for all.

The Dove campaign was born out of Unilever's concern that the brand had grown stale and boring. Working with the Ogilvy advertising agency, the company spent a year surveying customers and writing a report on beauty and self-esteem. They found that by defining beauty more broadly they could make Dove into a brand that more women would support. Sales increased wherever the campaign was used, and it became one of the past decade's more talked-about advertising initiatives.

Others have followed Dove's lead, tapping into the skepticism many people feel about media images and marketing. The editors of *Glamour* magazine, for example, won praise from many readers when they published photos of regular women (including nude shots) and ran a feature on the beauty of regular-sized women. Nike even published an advertisement that offered just a single image, of a large and muscled female posterior, and text in which a woman praises her curvy body.

Although Nike, *Glamour,* and others who use what's now called "reality branding" made waves, the original Dove campaign, which began in 2004, caused the biggest stir because it was the first to challenge stereotypes, and it revealed just how comfortable some people are expressing appearance-based bigotry. A typical negative reaction came from Chicago movie critic Richard Roeper, who couldn't get his mind around the idea of an advertiser suggesting that normal women are beautiful. "I find these Dove ads a little unsettling," he said. "If I want to see plump gals baring too much skin, I'll go to Taste of Chicago [an annual food festival], okay? When we're talking women in their underwear on billboards outside my living room windows, give me the fantasy babes, please. If that makes me sound superficial, shallow, and sexist—well yes, I'm a man."

What Roeper said and assumed about beauty, appearance, women, and men is sad and disappointing in many ways and is also a reflection of the prevailing attitude in the film industry, which he covers as a critic. In Hollywood, women are still often presented as the product of a remarkably immature male's fantasy. Some of this may have to do with habit, and the fact that only 10 percent of Hollywood directors are female. But the most obvious motivation for all this stereotyping is that movie critics, like Richard Roeper, believe that only a certain kind of beauty sells.

Unilever found that the opposite was true. The company reported double-digit sales growth as customers responded to the sight of regular-sized women who glowed with health and smiled with happiness. The Dove models seemed at ease with their figures, their faces, their skin, their hair, their *selves.* And the point of the ad campaign was not to arouse men like Roeper (although perhaps the culture has trained him to expect arousal from advertising) but to celebrate the 99.9 percent of women who are not shaped like today's runway models.

I know that Richard Roeper's comments represent an attitude that is pervasive and powerful. But I also like to hope that our culture can move away from the prejudice and ugliphobia they reflect. In America the brightest glimmer to support this hope can be seen in the first generation raised after the civil rights reforms of the 1960s, and the progress made by the women's movement in the 1970s with laws like the federal Title IX, which gave equal opportunity in education for women. Born between 1979 and 1990, which is after the civil rights era, members of this Generation Y (also called Millennials) have been exposed to more anti-bias, antibigotry messages than earlier generations. According to repeated surveys, they have turned out to be the least racist and most open-minded generation in history. They have a more inclusive sense of what makes a person appealing or attractive, and consistently say that good relationships are more essential to happiness than anything else.

Generation Y is also the group that produces and consumes a great deal of objectifying media and appears drawn to what's called a "hook-up" culture that emphasizes the value of porn-style appearance and sexual performance. For these reasons I have no illusions about a fast and sweeping rejection of ugliphobia that will suddenly make our society humane. But I can hope that young adults, adolescents, and children who already reject other kinds of prejudice would be receptive to the idea that appearance-based judgments are unfair and unjust too. Of course this would require anyone who has "gotten the message" to serve as a more effective parent, role model, and teacher.

If we want to pass on an inclusive, positive regard for all human beings and begin to change the culture, we must try to inoculate our own children against the sociogenic illness of ugliphobia. Many mothers have told me that they are afraid of how their daughters will be affected by a culture that focuses such an inordinate amount of attention on a woman's sexual appeal. One brought me a picture of her nine-year-old daughter and told me that her child's crooked teeth were a "saving grace" because her daughter looked and acted so sexually mature that she was afraid she would be abused. Her teeth, she hoped, would make her less appealing to anyone who might take advantage of her. Does this seem extreme? It isn't. I've had a few women in my practice who recalled being described in sexual terms by adults, even their fathers, when they were children and adolescents. This kind of attention—based entirely on sex appeal—creates confusion for parents and children in a culture where beauty and sexiness are often one and the same. How do you let a child know that she is appealing without making her feel sexualized?

I think you build a positive self-image in a child when you spend time with her and offer appreciation for all aspects of her character and personality, not just her appearance. Time together (not time spent shopping) is the essential element here, and it is especially important when kids have access to so much impersonal technology and entertainment. Kids who spend an excessive number of hours at the computer or watching DVDs don't learn to communicate well, or to be empathetic or compassionate. (This may be one cause of the "compassion deficit" in the young noted by Diane Levin of Wheelock College.) These are traits that can only be passed on in a relationship, and they are vital to a child's sense of well-being.

Of course, media will be part of a child's environment, and here we can counter appearance-based prejudice. Parents can decode the words and images—explaining that "real" people don't usually act like TV characters—and reframe the stories. *The Ugly Duckling* is a perfect example of a story in need of interpretation. It shows a "duckling" who is rejected for being unattractive. The happy ending comes when the "duckling" turns out to be a swan more beautiful than all the other birds. What's the message here? Is it that the scales will be balanced if you grow into someone more beautiful than everyone else? What if that doesn't happen? What if you turn out to be an ordinary duck? Don't you still have a right to be happy?

Small as this example may be, the reinterpretation of *The Ugly*

Duckling is the kind of lesson that can be reinforced throughout a child's life as she hears other stories about how a character is transformed—by new clothes, the wave of a fairy's wand, or some other means—and new-found beauty becomes her key to happiness. This kind of story ignores all the other pathways a child can take to happiness, offering instead a fantasy based on magic and prettiness. How would a child learn anything from this plot other than passivity, ugliphobia, and wishful thinking?

Throughout a child's life, an alert parent will find thousands of opportunities to discuss what the world offers as the keys to happiness—beauty, sexiness, consumerism, and so on—and offer alternatives. Since children watch what we do very closely (and may not listen much at all to what we say) we can best communicate our values by seeking balance in our own lives. Children inherit their parents' attitudes—joy, sadness, pride, shame, you name it—just as surely as they inherit eye color. If you've begun to accept yourself more fully, including all your Medusa parts, your kids will inherit that attitude of empathy and acceptance and become receptive to other parenting techniques that emphasize the development of their character, emotional intelligence, creativity, and critical thinking. Among my favorites are:

- **Focus the majority of your parenting on how your kids feel and what interests them, not on what they look like, or what the house looks like, or what the relatives and neighbors would think about your status.** I've got nothing against a neat house and clean kids, but remember that children know and feel where you put your priorities, and if most of your time goes into making things "look" good they'll do the same, often at the expense of being honest and in touch with their true feelings, talents, intelligence, and needs.
- **Choose toys that allow for flexibility of play and creativity.** The notion that the box a toy comes in is better for your child's development than the toy that came inside is often quite valid.

A big box can be a boat, a car, or a tent in a child's imagination. It provides open-ended play, which helps a child develop creativity and problem solving.

• **Establish a "no-tolerance policy" for cruelty.** I'm not a big fan of rigid rules, but this is one I endorse. It is essential to creating an emotionally safe environment and for a child's evolving empathy for herself and others.

• **Resist gender stereotyping within the family system.** Men can cook and women can pump their own gas. Women can push a lawn mower, men can change diapers.

• **Monitor your kids' exposure to media and talk to them in an age-appropriate way about what they see and hear, especially when they are exposed to suggestive or pornographic material.** In a world saturated by such images it makes no sense to ignore them. Instead we need to help children to understand the techniques used by the media to influence how to feel and think. It can be very helpful to tell a child how *you* feel when you are exposed to certain images and invite a discussion.

• **Share the secrets of the marketplace.** When you shop, talk about the difference between needs and wants, and the methods marketers use to manipulate us. This kind of conversation—about how retailers and merchandisers manipulate our desires, works very well with adolescents and adults. A good example from my own life came when I talked with a young friend who was puzzled about shopping for gifts. He felt conflicted about how much he was supposed to spend in order to show he cared for someone and about finding just the right styles to be "in fashion." A five-minute chat about how retailers create anxiety and a false sense of urgency in customers— and how he might be happier following his own quirky taste— helped him feel happier and more competent.

• **Be honest about your own struggle.** It's not only okay but essential to share your own feelings and say "I don't know" when you are stumped by a problem or don't understand something. When we let kids know that we're struggling to think our way through an issue or make peace with our feelings, they learn that being uncomfortable is okay and that you don't find your balance by making a purchase.

- **Teach independent thought and encourage your child's free will.** This means letting go of saying "Because I'm the parent, that's why," and actually answering your child's questions. If we bully children we run the risk of them becoming bullies themselves or of watching them overreact in the extreme in order to assert their autonomy.

- **Help your child balance his autonomy with empathy for others.** Self-determination doesn't equal obnoxious self-centeredness. When we treat others as we would like to be treated (remember the Golden Rule?) we make every encounter more genuine, humane, and nourishing for all.

- **Advocate for anti-bullying policies in your schools.** These policies make schools safer and more effective. (Researcher Dewey Cornell of the University of Virginia recently published a study that showed academic performance improves when bullying is not an option.)

These few concepts suggest only a foundation that can support an endlessly varied approach to raising children. (You'll devise many more as you make the art of parenting your own.) The point is to raise a child who is more resilient, openhearted, and less in need of the big psychological defenses that make it hard to have relationships. Defenses—denying your feelings, judging yourself and others harshly, isolating yourself, controlling others, and so on—evolve in response to shame. Shame recedes when we are able to accept ourselves more fully.

In every day and throughout our lives, we can find ways to pass on the spirit of acceptance and gratitude that is the opposite of the ugliphobia and bigotry that dominate our culture. I try to do this whether I am facing a bank teller at my local branch or talking on the phone with a customer service representative halfway around the world. It can become a habit, one that's reinforced by an endless stream of positive experiences that come when you offer someone your empathy and they return it, in kind. This is the type of sociogenic process that just might change your life in dramatic ways, and make the world just a little more beautiful.

APPENDIX: SPEAK OUT

In April 2009 I joined the million-plus member Internet forum
All Facebook Females Unite in One Group and posted the following
message:

> I'm writing a book about a topic that has plagued me my whole life . . .
> feeling ugly and believing I'm ugly. I'd really love your feedback on this
> topic, because I know I'm not the only one . . . in fact, I don't know anyone,
> especially any woman, who doesn't believe there's something ugly about
> her. If you want to write to me privately about this, you can send an email to
> me . . . Or you can post here. Either would be terrific help with my research
> . . . and maybe we can support each other in the process.
>
> Thanks

My initial post was purposely open-ended. It assumed that this feeling
is common and invited respondents to reflect and offer very personal
replies. They came, by the hundreds, from every corner of the globe, from
men as well as women, from people of all ages and social backgrounds.
In some cases the dialogues that developed provoked conflict. For example,
my suggestion that the word "ugly" might be reinterpreted in a more
positive way was met by sharp criticism from people who believed the
word was too powerful, and dangerous, to be appropriated for anything

good. At other times in the discussion participants were mocked rather cruelly by interlopers, most of whom seemed to be boys and young men. But for the most part the posts were sincere and heartfelt and they confirmed what I have discovered in my research: People all over the world suffer from the fear of ugliness. It is used everywhere by bullies who want to control and abuse others. It limits our lives, and it is such a taboo subject that people welcome the chance to discuss it safely.

The entries in this appendix were selected because they represent the range of contributions, lending support for my thesis and for anyone who struggles with the ugly issue. They have been edited for spelling. Web slang and emoticons have been removed. I have tried to maintain, as well as possible, the intent of the contributor. As you read them you may notice that the writers often say that they "feel ugly" when they are, in fact, experiencing loss, abandonment, neglect, and even abuse in various relationships. We often believe we are ugly, and even say we are ugly, when instead, we are suffering from rejection by others who treat us as if we are not worthy. Feeling ugly is also associated with normal bodily changes such as menstruation, pregnancy, aging, and surgeries.

This appendix, which comprises less than 10 percent of the responses to my initial query, may also serve as an antidote for our feelings of isolation and as evidence that, sadly, the fear of ugliness and the bigotry and suffering that go with it, are not confined to any one place, culture, gender, age group, or class of people. They affect us all.

FROM THE FACEBOOK FORUM

Question: When do you feel ugly?

Responses

There are certain days where I feel like I don't look my best and that always gets me in a bad mood. Sometimes I'm so excited to wear something and I think I look great until someone makes a rude remark. Then I feel like everyone is out to get me. I'll never understand why I'll feel this way but I feel like I'll never find that answer. Feeling ugly has always plagued me and I've always hoped that one day, I can ignore that feeling and be able to express myself in any way I want!

In the morning when I wake up.

I feel ugly a lot of the time. I was told growing up I was fat and ugly and no one would want me . . . as I gained weight over the years and now hitting past-mid-forties . . . I feel so ugly and inadequate sometimes . . . war wounds from having babies, surgery scar . . . I wonder if all women wonder why others got blessed with certain attributes and why some of us lack. Then there are days I think hey I don't look bad for forty-six and a grammie . . . I guess a lot of others are better at hiding feelings than me . . . I like transparency.

I hope this doesn't come out the wrong way but anyway. I used to worry about it but I feel annoyed now that I spent so much time worrying about it and feeling inferior/insecure. All that time feeling crap about something that is so insignificant as how I look or how people judge something I have little control over. Look after yourself yes, but do it for yourself so you are healthy.

I have really bad skin and pimples and scars on my face from them.
Sometimes I would feel so insecure I would think anyone who looked at
me/talked to me, all they would see is how ugly I was but then I realized that
it's a silly thing to worry about. If I start to feel like that I consciously decide
that I am going to put my energy into something I find that is more important.

I also just want to say that there are a lot of industries that make a lot of
money out of making people feel insecure about themselves. Cosmetic industry, magazines, makeup, gyms—basically marketing for most things is to
make you feel as though you really need what they have and anything related
to looks . . . the worse they make people feel about themselves the more money
they are likely to make. Stuff them!

I am in my late fifties, and I feel ugly in the morning. I'm no spring chicken
so I don't expect to look as fresh as the morning dew when I get up, but I
make it a point never to leave the house without makeup on, and the rest of
the day I'm good as new. Bad hair days also make me feel ugly and putting
on weight is another one so I try my best to maintain it. Sometimes we
cannot help it, as in Malaysia we celebrate four festivals and that's when
I go on an eating spree and tell myself I'll diet another day so I have clothes
in S, M, and L. Ugly is also hair turning white at the roots and I hate it when
the wind blows and the roots are exposed. I have to color my roots every
three weeks to feel good. I'm blessed with good genes and do not look
my age so other than that, I feel good most of the time.

I am nineteen. I have felt ugly when I was little. I was bullied in school and I have always been self-aware of what I look like because I don't want anyone to think bad about me or call me names. The worst time I felt ugly was two years ago I was going on my first holiday out of England with my first boyfriend who is now my ex. Before we went away he told me I need to tone up and lose weight before we go so I looked good in my bikini even though I only was eight stone already. I didn't feel very comfortable in my bikini that holiday. Last year I stopped eating because of my ex kept saying I need to lose weight. I did end up finishing the relationship with him. I am now eating and my confidence is slow coming back up. I still don't feel comfortable about myself sometimes but my new boyfriend shows me the love I need and is making [me] more confident as time goes by.

Even if everything else is perfect I feel like a troll if I don't wash my hair. Or if I'm wearing an outfit that doesn't go well together. I know it sounds superficial, but it's more about feeling inadequate than being pretty. It's my old high school fear of not being good enough, and you know in high school you have to look good enough to be good enough.

This probably isn't as good of an answer as some people, but I feel pretty ugly all the time. I'm pretty tall for a girl, really wide shoulders, no butt, Chun-Li thighs, and to top it all off, I'm pregnant. Plus I'm in a relationship with a really hot guy who's not my baby's father. He never says anything bad about the way I look or anything good, really . . . but I feel like, compared to the other girls he's been with, I'm just a fat, football-player looking man-woman

and I feel like I have to keep my pregnancy a secret around his friends, so I
can never be Cute Pregnant Girlfriend. I'll just have to settle for Fat Girlfriend.

An easier question would be when do I not feel ugly? Most of the time I feel
hopeless and completely unattractive.

I don't FEEL ugly, I am ugly. But I am what I am and that's just something
I'm growing to accept. You always hear people saying "No one's ugly, everyone's
beautiful in their own way," but come on now . . . You can't notice when someone is "pretty" without noticing another is "ugly". If pretty exists, then ugly has
to too.

When I do anything that validates all the terrible things my mom said to
me as a child and young adult. When I feel I've failed as a provider, parent, or
partner. Rarely ever is it a feeling of actual physical unattractiveness. It's the
kind on the inside.

I feel ugly when I allow other people's opinions of me (from the past)
penetrate me and take over what I know about myself. More so when I'm in a
place where I feel people will be more "likely" to say the things I heard so
many years ago, so many years in a row. If I allow the thoughts/memories to
take over my mind, I'm a hot mess. I feel ugly when I allow it.

I ALWAYS feel ugly, well, not really feel, just I AM UGLY. I'm really insecure
now and constantly feel ugly but I have just got used to it and only look in the
mirror when I'm doing my hair, makeup, and making sure my clothes match.

I feel pretty all the time. No kidding.

I feel ugly all the time. I even get really nasty comments because I'm your classic envied person—tall and slim naturally, can eat what I like when I like. But there are bad sides to it. I'm not curvy, have no breasts or hips. I bloat because I'm so small when I eat much my body does not like it and I end up looking six months pregnant. I suffered from terrible pregnancies because my body can't handle them. I now have a six-inch scar snaking round my abdomen due to ectopic pregnancies. For years I have struggled with my body, wanting to be a size twelve to fourteen, and it will not happen. So for all those women out there who are that size, embrace your curves because that's beauty.

I think if someone tells you that you are fat and ugly often enough, you start to believe it yourself.

It's like I am invisible, and only a few people notice me . . . It is said that beauty is not what life is about, but for God sake, every day proves the opposite.

I have been out to the shops, strutted my stuff like I am the queen of good looks. Then got home and thought "What blind animal put this outfit together?" Jeez, I'm a stuffed ham wrapped in cloth. Depressing. I always feel more attractive when I have no mirrors.

Okay, so I'm a guy and I'll tell you when I feel ugly. I'm usually confident with my body, but sometimes when I go through stress I start scratching my face and I look in the mirror and pick at any small bump or white dot I can see. Then there are many scratch marks, and it looks like I have acne. I then feel so ugly that I stay in my room and wait till it looks better and the wounds have healed.

I've read almost all of these posts, and I've been thinking very hard about what I will say. What it comes down to is that all the people who think they are ugly are the most beautiful people I have seen! Both inside and out! And I do agree, if you aren't happy with the way you look, go and change it, BUT don't become dependent on these changes.

When we are happy, everything is beautiful.

I definitely struggle with this . . . it bugs me when the "solutions" involve purchasing a product (new makeup, haircut, clothing) and not other ways of appreciating and nurturing oneself. This practice seems to imply that some goo in a tube is the key when really, there's so much more to it than that. (Ironically, many of the most beautiful people I know use few "beauty" products. I think my partner is incredibly stunning and his main personal care items are bar soap and toothpaste.)

Would it be more productive to alter the meaning of a word rather than ignore its use? If we started referring to ourselves as ugly, would the word lose its effect? I have heard "fea" used as a term of endearment (Spanish speaking, literally translates to "ugly"). Perhaps a page could be taken from this book? Change the culture around our language? When I was young, "sick" referred to having an illness, or something gross. If someone shouted "THAT'S SICK" it meant that they were horrified. Today, the same term is used to refer to something great!

Well, I feel ugly every day as people stare at me and see me like a monster. Also, many children at school laugh at me constantly.

I'm only a thin little girl 'cause I'm tall, I don't have boobs or a butt (like my mummy). And I have moles on me. Sometimes I feel insecure about pimples or the fact that I have bad front teeth at the top from when my brother smashed my head into the table when we were drinking juice as kids. People always say that you can't be a real woman unless you have curves. But there are a lot of smaller-sized girls out there who are real women, too. It's just we are more compact, and a little more boney. God made you for a reason, model your own body type and show girls that are younger than you that have the same body type how to be comfortable being their selves. We are all natural born models! PS: I have as much cellulite as any other girl in the world, that's all a myth!

I have to wonder though, is this just a girl thing or do guys feel the same way but maybe just don't talk about it as much? I feel ugly when I'm around people I know are prettier than me and then all my insecurities flare up. I'm suddenly utterly conscious of any spot, any hair out of place, and anything I don't find pleasant about myself. Lots of people say they think about it when they wake up, but it's not till I sit up, and look in the mirror and do my best to look nice, feel semi-pleased with myself and then step outdoors into the eyes of others that I feel "ugly." I wonder if women have always been this way.

Did all of us jump in this discussion with the assumption that ugly was associated with looks? You are too right, ugly can be associated with a characteristic or an action. Hate is ugly. Unhappiness is ugly. Have you ever seen someone who has been transformed from a hateful and unhappy person into a content and loving person? Their appearance changes! Lines of disapproval, worry, sorrow, doubt, etc., are erased and a beautiful person emerges—no matter what they look like (big nose, acne scars, crooked ears, crossed eyes) they are transformed. So all of us who are sitting on the ugly chair, stop staring at yourselves in disapproval and wishing you looked different—accept who you are and become beautiful overnight!

Wow ... I was a skinny little girl but was called fat ass all the time. I was almost anorexic at sixteen and always thought I was fat ... I am now forty-six also and the funny thing is, now I really am fat, really, really overweight and I don't give a damn, it seemed to almost become a rebellious thing NOT to be thin ... although I need to do something about it now as it is not healthy. I have problems because of it, e.g. sleep apnea and bad back ... but isn't it funny how we are still a product of our childhood, don't parents have a lot to answer for ... as for feeling ugly, I don't usually feel ugly unless I see myself in a mirror ... then I kind of freak .

I would also like to offer some insight into a man's self-image, as a number of y'all have expressed curiosity as to what we think. Personally, there are times where I see a guy who is better looking, stronger, or more talented than me, and I truly do feel I am ugly by comparison. I feel the pressure of a conflicting self-image at the gym, while watching TV, and while reading magazines . . . I'm not overly strong or buff, and most of the men presented in the media are. It is even more difficult for us to address these issues, as our society encourages men to hold in our emotions and personal images. (Unless these emotions are "manly," such as anger . . .). We suffer a similar fate with our self-image, however, we don't talk about it . . . we aren't "supposed" to care about that "stuff" . . . so shh.

When people around me said that I am not pretty enough, just ordinary.

When I was a girl I used to get called frog eyes and chicken legs so I don't think that helped. There are worst things in life though.

I would have to say that I FEEL ugly when I have displayed an angry out-burst complete with swearing, stomping feet, crying, and screaming. These displays are extremely rare for me but when they happen I am ashamed— not for being angry but for showing my anger in such a fashion.

My experience of depression tells me that not attending to my physical appearance makes me feel worse. There is a lot of benefit in putting on makeup and feeling that I look nice. If I told myself I was ugly, I'd feel a lot worse.

When I'm tired, when I look at pictures of models, etc. in magazines, or see gorgeous girls around, or, go shopping and realize all the sizes that exist below mine. Or worst of all, if my boyfriend compliments some girl/celebrity. I should be confident enough to deal with that because it shouldn't make me feel any less good about myself, but I really let it ruin my mood.

All the time. I feel ugly all the time!! It's only when I've got a thick layer of foundation . . . my hair poker straight and a fresh layer of fake tan on . . . When I look in the mirror without these things on . . . it's like it's not my face . . . ??

Just wanted to remind everyone that no matter how ugly or unattractive you may be feeling on any given day, try to remember that it honestly doesn't matter what the hell you look like. Try to take a second to step out of the small picture and into the big one. Looks are so fading. You will inevitably get old and your body will change. That's why it is so incredibly important to love who you are as a person, not just certain features or characteristics. There is something in all of us that is intrinsically you, and only you, and it has nothing to do with how you look or what you wear or what kind of car you drive or how funny you are. Try to get in touch with that part of you. That's who you really are. I know it sounds far-fetched, but that's only because we are conditioned to think all the other things in life matter. They don't. Don't waste precious time feeling sorry for yourself. There are people out there going through unbelievably difficult things, that would love to be in someone else's shoes if all they had to worry about was that they felt ugly. I'm not saying to never feel ugly, but rather, that when you do, shake yourself off, and say, it doesn't matter. I like who I am. That's all that counts.

I went to school with an "ugly" person. Bad eyesight, improper hygiene, cleft palate, club foot, speech impediment. She had everything against her and on top of all those problems, she did not look very feminine: broad hands, flat features, clumsy, a bit overweight. Kids made fun of her all the time. I chose to be her friend all through school. I also chose to take her out of my friendship about twenty-five years ago after school was done and I'm very sorry but it was because I felt smothered by her. Did she "know" she was "ugly"? I believe so. Did she try to become "un-ugly"? All the time. Could she really change the way she was? On a lot of things, sure, but basic looks, without surgery, no. I hope she was able to accept who she was and enjoy her life. I hope she had kids and a man to love and appreciate her. If you see this, you know who you are. I'm sorry I ever ditched you and if you would have me back in your life again I would feel honored.

I feel ugly until I spend an hour on my hair and makeup, picking out the perfect clothes and matching shoes. Even then I only feel pretty if someone tells me I look pretty. Every time I look in the mirror, I see something new wrong. When I spend time with my female friends or stand next to my sister, I feel ugly. When I flip through a magazine or turn on the TV, I feel ugly.

I feel ugly when I've got roots! But this is soon resolved by a trip to my hairdresser. Say no to grey!

I feel like people are scanning me up and down and thinking of flaws.

When I was in middle and high school I was always either bullied, or the outsider . . . lol, I guess it made me extremely conscious about myself; because I'm Hispanic, I always felt different and uglier than all the other blue-eyed, blond-looking models that seemed to have no hair out of place. However, now, I've gained a lot more confidence in myself—I guess makeup and a straightener had something to do with it as well. Now, the only time I feel ugly, or conscious of my looks, is when I'm around someone that really cares about their looks without being "dressed up"—I guess it makes me feel as if they're criticizing me.

I feel ugly when I get rejected by a guy . . . I've never had a boyfriend and sometimes I feel there will never be anyone right out there for me.

I am an overweight person—so of course it's in my face all the time—skinny this, model that . . . you know? I've battled insecurity about it since my teenage years when I was anorexic. Over the years I've come to terms with my weight and how I approach managing it (although it still manages me most times).

I feel so ugly when I put on clothes I don't like and when I feel so unwanted in the place I am in.

Every day. I hate looking in the mirror because I think I look ugly. I hate trying on clothes and I'm only twenty but my stomach looks like I'm three months pregnant but no matter how much exercise I do it won't go away. So, my clothes end up making me fat and all the media and celebrity hype of "thin, beautiful people" make me even sadder.

I have a weight issue ... I am much heavier than I should be. It does not restrict me from being active and doing the things I like to do. Built for comfort not for speed ... I have a lot of great qualities but they will never take the time to allow me to show them because they can't or won't get over what I look like ... as well as we could get along, great, but it won't go any further because what will their friends and family say if their choice isn't "perfect"? They give into the fear of seeming less to the world. When repeatedly I get rejected, any confidence is gone and at that point it starts to affect all areas of my life not just dating. I try hard not to let it but repeatedly I let the opinion of some complete stranger who once I got to know, I probably would not even want to be with, define who I am ... that is ugly.

I feel ugly when I'm making decisions to make other people happy. I feel ugly, unlovable, uncared for, and unwanted.

Not sure. I don't feel ugly per se, but more insecure. Weight is a big issue in my family. As a kid I was a bit chubby, I remember my dad saying "Are you sure you want to eat those?" once when we were eating pancakes. Which is kind of a big blow in your self-esteem at that age. My mom is obese, she has made fun of thin/slim girls for as long as I can remember. And that's what makes me insecure about how I look. I've lost about eighteen kilograms (which is around thirty-five pounds I think) in one and a half years, and I kind of have mixed feelings about. I like how I am now, but knowing that my mom makes comments about me, the "GIRL, you look horrible, you need to EAT cause your bones are sticking out" comments, doesn't make me feel good about myself.

When I was fifteen I felt ugly. A guy came to me and he told me he saw me on TV. I was happy thinking maybe he liked me. But he continued—"in the movie *Friday the 13th*." When I realized it's about zombies my whole life was ruined.

I feel the ugliest (physically speaking) when I'm with my family. The things they said have been so cruel, it will NEVER go away. I feel the prettiest with complete strangers, they've always been nicer to me.

I feel ugly after the hikes my mum takes me on. I get tired because they're mega long, and then she calls me unfit afterwards. But it's not really me thinking I'm ugly, it's me thinking I'm inadequate, really. I'm not fat, I'm happy with how I look (minus spots and slight wobbliness on my legs).

Right now. Almost every day for the past few months. My marriage has failed. I REALLY didn't see it coming. I feel like I'm self-destructing.

Hi, I came across your discussion after endless hours on the Internet searching for answers. I feel like dying, I'm on the verge of suicide and I really can't think of anyone to talk to. I can't talk to anyone about this. It's so horrible, because I have to stay alive for my family, I couldn't do that to them. The thought of my parents walking in on my dead body on the floor makes me recoil in horror. I don't know who you are, and I don't know if you could help me. I don't know if you will respond and I don't even know why I'm writing this to you. I'm just reaching out in the dark because no one can help me and I am so backed up against a wall I literally cannot breathe. I've felt hideous my entire life. I literally don't leave the house at times and stay in my room all day, not even going downstairs to eat because I am so disgusted in my appearance. I posted a picture up of myself today and I got so many negative responses, it felt like someone reached inside my stomach and ripped out my internal organs. I'm nineteen years old and I've never had a boyfriend and have iso-lated myself from friends and family. The funny thing is, that when I'm out in public I've had people approach me, I get asked out sometimes, guys stare at me and people even tell me that I'm pretty. I don't understand. I can't get over this horrible feeling. My mom is the only person in the world I trust, and I can't even talk to her about this because it hurts her when I do. And I don't want to hurt her no more. When I pour my heart out to my friends I feel like I just make the situation awkward, and they never know what to say to me. And I don't blame them. I'm trying to cry silently as I type this, I'm literally trying not to burst into tears and scream. I can't take this anymore . . . I believe I am ugly because of the way I have been treated my whole life. I can't stand to see myself in photos or on video cameras. I feel like I look so deformed and I'm too ugly to even be with people. I often get angry at my parents for being born . . . I feel ignored by the world. I was picked on as a child for the way I looked as well. I'm planning on getting plastic surgery, even though I know its shallow, it will be the only thing that will help me. I often feel invisible. I know killing myself isn't the right thing to do but I honestly see no point in living. Plastic surgery is all I can think about. I can't look in the mirror without pushing my nose up and pulling my eyes tight. The dark circles and shadows aren't what bugs me but it's the actual permanent puffiness I have under my eyes. Ever since I was a kid I had people asking me if I got enough sleep last night, or why I look so tired, or why I am wearing dark makeup under my eyes. You can imagine how painful it is to hear that as just a child. I *always* look tired no matter what, and I feel at my age I shouldn't have to worry about this. If they look this bad now, imagine how they will look ten, twenty years from now? I don't think that "ugly" people don't deserve a fulfilling life, but I feel ugly people have it so much harder compared to those who are good-looking. I fear if I ever get involved with a guy, he will constantly be looking at prettier girls and thinking about them. I am attending university and I feel invisible. In high school, it is a much smaller community and you are acknowledged as being a part of it, but now that I am here in university I feel like I haven't met any friends because I'm not pretty enough. I have never felt so alone and neglected in my entire life. I feel as though I'm floating by. I am on academic probation because last year I missed so much class because of the problems I have with my appearance and leaving the house. I am seeing a counselor at school and she is helping me sort some things out but at the back of my mind I can't stop thinking of getting my nose busted into shape and the godforsaken tumorous curse removed from under my eyes. When I stand in certain lighting and catch a glimpse of my reflection I am horrified at how bad my bags look, it literally looks like my eyes are melting . . . I feel like I am really stuck here, because getting surgery is so unattainable for me right now as money is an issue and a part of me is telling me not to go through with it. Yet I feel if I don't get it, I will never be happy. I will never be able to accept myself, because the face I have been born with is unacceptable. I will never accept it. I hate everything about it.

I feel the most ugly everyday because of past experiences of my so-called "friends" calling me fat, they told me I had double chins and that I need to lose weight when all I weighed was 130 at five-four (sounds pretty normal). And (family) would constantly tell me when I would eat that I'm too fat or I shouldn't be eating and then when I would confront them about it they would say, I'm being too emotional and about the prom thing me and my date had literally just arrived at the hotel and on the way to the elevator some girl who was with her mother and date just looked over and started laughing and saying I was ugly. I was shocked because how could she be so bold to say that to me and then later on that night I had to deal with my best friend's date telling me, "damn, you got a big forehead," it was all too much for me and those memories will never leave me.

My mother was raised with that fifties mentality about how looks are all you have as an asset. My mother would tell me things as I was growing up such as, "Oh, is that what you are wearing?" Which, of course, would make me self doubt. She would continue to add, "Well, dresses make you look fat." I was only eight or nine when she started that mind game with me. As I got older, my mother would say passive-aggressive things about my weight. Then she'd say things to imply that no one loves me, only her. She would go to lengths to prove it by manipulating my friends, and sabotaging my relationships with boys, through psychological manipulation. She would put suggestions in my head at crucial moments. She made sure that my self-image was not full of confidence, but full of doubt. It was almost like she was jealous of my youthfulness, and was competing with me, by showing me how thin she was compared to me, how attractive she was, and that if I just lost weight, I could be that attractive. As a teenager, and then a young adult, her voice could still be heard by me, every time I was about to go out on a date. As an adult, it has caused me to feel so insecure that it has interfered with my relationships. I could never have believed I was loved, because I couldn't believe that they saw me as attractive, because I don't believe I am pretty. I feel ugly most of the time. That insecurity created arguments and those would lead to break-ups.

Anyway the thing seems to be that I feel ugly when someone treats me in a lousy way. Especially if it comes from males. And yes, I feel ugly every time I open any fashion magazine or start watching a movie with beautiful Hollywood babes living their perfect life. I have been putting on some weight in the past couple of years and I feel ugly when I can't find clothes big enough from my favorite stores. And when I feel fat, I feel ugly. Most of the time when I see myself naked just standing front of the mirror I feel ugly. I'm far away from beauty queens like Marilyn Monroe. But as soon as I get my stuffed bra, loose clothing, and makeup on, at least a part of it goes away. And btw, thanks for asking. I think this analyzing did some good to me.

Please excuse me for my bad English but I am French educated, so please don't laugh at my mistakes. I saw your post in one of the groups ... All my life I have been a "big girl," I am ninety kilos and as for my height I am 1.68 cm [five foot six] (by the way I am twenty-one years old); but I never had a problem with my weight and my looks. It never used to bother me even though my parents would use harsh comments like "you look like a cow" thinking that it would make me lose weight; but still I never listened. Anyways, three years ago I met a guy who I loved tremendously, I gave him everything I had from my love, to money, support; my parents hated him and threatened that if I ever saw him again they wouldn't send me to Italy in order to continue my studies in opera (I am an opera singer). So I used to sneak out and lie whenever I was able to for the last year and a half just to be with him and see him. I loved him and I knew he loved me. He never told me that he had a problem with my weight and that he loved me for who I am and our sexual life was quite good.

In the last two years, he told me that he had this fantasy of having a threesome, me, him, and another girl; I couldn't say no because he used to threaten me that he would leave me, so I accepted just for the sake of our relationship and because I loved him. Whenever we would meet a girl and she would accept, I would take her aside and tell her that it was not my idea and I don't want to do it (the girls understood, and they would tell my bf that they changed their minds, he never knew it was because I was talking to them). One month ago he met a girl and she was more than willing to join us. Unfortunately I was not able to talk to her and tell her the whole story. Tonight was suppose to be the night where would do it and I told him NO, that I wasn't willing to do such a thing. He started hitting me and told me that a threesome was the most important thing in his life and just how I knew he was going to end it, he told me that for the past three years he never enjoyed our sexual relationship with me because I was fat and couldn't do the moves and positions he liked; he even topped it by saying "All of the girls I slept with before you were much better than you, you're just fat." Now not only do I not trust guys anymore but I've never felt more disgusted about who I am and what I look like. I feel that I'm nothing but some sort of fat garbage who never even deserved to be with him and that he deserves someone much better than me physically-wise.

SOURCES

Ugly As Sin is the product of a decades-long interest in the subject and years of work with psychotherapy clients and students at Empire State College who have studied a wide range of topics from group dynamics to domestic violence. It is informed by hundreds of sources including academic journals, books, and articles from the popular press. Those offered here are among the most relevant and would be valuable for those interested in further reading.

On the subject of ugliness as a historical and cultural phenomenon:

Berlyne, D. E. *Aesthetics and Psychobiology*. New York: Appelton-Century-Crofts, 1971.

Berry, J. W., and Jean Phinney, eds. *Immigrant Youth in Cultural Transition: Acculturation, Identity, and Adaptation Across National Contexts*. Mahwah, NJ: Erlbaum, 2006.

Bourdieu, Pierre. *Distinction: A Social Critique of the Judgment of Taste*. Cambridge, MA: Harvard University Press, 1984.

Botting, Kate, and Douglas Botting. *Sex Appeal: The Art and Science of Sexual Attraction*. New York: St. Martin's Press, 1996.

Eco, Umberto, ed. *History of Beauty*. New York: Rizzoli, 2005.

————, ed. *On Ugliness*. New York: Rizzoli, 2007.

Garber, Marjorie, and Nancy J. Vickers. *The Medusa Reader*. New York: Routledge, 2003.

Haiken, Elizabeth. *Venus Envy: A History of Cosmetic Surgery*. Baltimore, MD: Johns Hopkins University Press, 1997.

Hochschild, Arlie Russell. *The Commercialization of Intimate Life*. Berkeley: University of California Press, 2003.

Kullick, Don, and Anne Meneley, eds. *Fat: The Anthropology of an Obsession*. New York: Jeremy P. Tarcher, 2005.

Miller, Ian William. *The Anatomy of Disgust*. Cambridge, MA: Harvard University Press, 1997.

Orbach, Susie. *Bodies*. New York: Picador, 2009.

Patzer, Gordon L. *Looks: Why They Matter More Than You Ever Imagined*. New York: AMACOM, 2008.

Stark, Rodney, and William Sims Bainbridge. *Religion, Deviance, and Social Control*. New York: Routledge, 1996.

Wright, Charlotte. *Plain and Ugly Janes: The Rise of the Ugly Woman in Contemporary American Fiction*. New York: Garland Pub., 2000.

Women and the issue of appearance and sexuality:

Brumberg, Joan Jacobs. *The Body Project: An Intimate History of American Girls*. New York: Random House, 1997.

Cash, Thomas F., and Thomas Pruzinsky, eds. *Body Images: Development, Deviance, and Change*. New York: Guilford Press, 1990.

Durham, M. Gigi. *The Lolita Effect: The Media Sexualization of Girls and What We Can Do About It*. New York: The Overlook Press, 2008.

Etcoff, Nancy. *Survival of the Prettiest: The Science of Beauty*. New York: Doubleday, 1999.

Hesse-Biber, Sharlene Nagy. *Am I Thin Enough Yet? The Cult of Thinness and the Commercialization of Identity.* New York: Oxford University Press, 1996.

Pipher, Mary. *Hunger Pains: From Fad Diets to Eating Disorders—What Every Woman Needs to Know About Food, Dieting, and Self-Concept.* Holbrook, MA: Adams Pub., 1995.

Tannenbaum, Leora. *Slut! Growing Up Female With a Bad Reputation.* New York: Seven Stories Press, 1999.

Issues relating to the economy, the media, and appearance:

Barber, Benjamin R. *Con$umed: How Markets Corrupt Children, Infantilize Adults, and Swallow Citizens Whole.* New York: W. W. Norton & Co., 2007.

Bourdieu, Pierre. *Acts of Resistance: Against the Tyranny of the Market.* New York: The New Press, 1999.

Gimlin, Debra L. *Body Work: Beauty and Self-Image in American Culture.* Berkeley: University of California Press, 2001.

Hall, Ann C., and Mardia J. Bishop, eds. *Pop-porn: Pornography in American Culture.* Westport, CT: Praeger, 2007.

Levin, Diane E., and Jean Kilbourne. *So Sexy So Soon: The New Sexualized Childhood and What Parents Can Do to Protect Kids.* New York: Ballantine Books, 2008.

Wykes, Maggie, and Barrie Gunter. *The Media and Body Image: If Looks Could Kill.* Thousand Oaks, CA: SAGE, 2005.

Issues in psychology and emotional development:

Beck, Aaron T., and Gary Emery with Ruth L. Greenberg. *Anxiety Disorders and Phobias: A Cognitive Perspective.* Cambridge, MA: Basic Books, 2005.

Brennan, Teresa. *The Transmission of Affect.* Ithaca, NY: Cornell University Press, 2004.

Ciarrochi, Joseph, Joseph P. Forgas, and John D. Mayer, eds. *Emotional Intelligence in Everyday Life*. Philadelphia, PA: Psychology Press, 2001.

Forsyth, Donelson R. *Group Dynamics*. Pacific Grove, CA: Brooks/Cole, 1990.

Goleman, Daniel. *Emotional Intelligence*. New York: Bantam Books, 1995.

———. *Social Intelligence: The New Science of Human Relationships*. New York: Bantam Books, 2006.

Hirigoyen, Marie-France. *Stalking the Soul: Emotional Abuse and the Erosion of Identity*. New York: Helen Marx Books, 2000.

Levine, Peter A., and Maggie Kline. *Trauma Through a Child's Eyes: Awakening the Ordinary Miracle of Healing*. Berkeley: North Atlantic Books, 2006.

Miller, Alice. *Thou Shalt Not Be Aware: Society's Betrayal of the Child*. New York: Farrar, Straus & Giroux, 1984.

Mook, Douglas. *Classic Experiments in Psychology*. Westport, CT: Greenwood Press, 2004.

Rose, Peter I., ed. *Socialization and the Life Cycle*. New York: St. Martin's Press, 1979.

Shawn, Allen. *Wish I Could Be There: Notes from a Phobic Life*. New York: Viking, 2007.

Wegner, Daniel M. *The Illusion of Conscious Will*. Cambridge, MA: MIT Press, 2002.

———. *The Lucifer Effect: Understanding How Good People Turn Evil*. New York: Random House, 2007.

Zimbardo, Philip G. *The Psychology of Imprisonment: Privation, Power and Pathology*. Stanford, CA: Stanford University Press, 1972.

More on healing and developing the self:

Gardner, James, and Arthur H. Bell. *Phobias and How to Overcome Them:*

Understanding and Beating Your Fears. Franklin Lakes, NJ: New Page Books, 2005.

Gold, Taro. *Living Wabi Sabi: The True Beauty of Your Life*. Kansas City, MO: Andrews McMeel, 2004.

Gough, Russell Wayne. *Character Is Destiny: The Value of Personal Ethics in Everyday Life*. Rocklin, CA: Forum, 1998.

Kaufman, Gershen. *Shame: The Power of Caring*. Rochester, VT: Schenkman Books, 1992.

Kaufman, Gershen, and Lev Raphael. *Dynamics of Power: Fighting Shame and Building Self-esteem*. Rochester, VT: Schenkman Books, 1991.

Kessler, David A. *The End of Overeating: Taking Control of the Insatiable American Appetite*. Emmaus, PA: Rodale, 2009.

Kreamer, Anne. *Going Gray: What I Learned About Beauty, Sex, Work, Motherhood, Authenticity, and Everything Else That Really Matters*. New York: Little, Brown and Co., 2007.

Nelson, Todd D. *The Psychology of Prejudice*. Boston: Pearson Allyn & Bacon, 2006.

Pipher, Mary Bray. *Another Country: Navigating the Emotional Terrain of Our Elders*. New York: Riverhead Books, 1999.

———. *Reviving Ophelia: Saving the Selves of Adolescent Girls*. New York: Putnam, 1994.

———. *The Shelter of Each Other: Rebuilding Our Families*. New York: G. P. Putnam's Sons, 1996.

Ponterotto, Joseph G., et al. *Preventing Prejudice: A Guide for Counselors, Educators, and Parents*. Thousand Oaks, CA: SAGE, 2006.

Schwartz, Pepper. *Prime: Adventures and Advice on Sex, Love and the Sensual Years*. New York: HaperCollins, 2007.

Vaughan, Susan C. *The Talking Cure: The Science Behind Psychotherapy*. New York: Henry Holt, 1998.

Viorst, Judith. *Necessary Losses: The Loves, Illusions, Dependencies and Impossible Expectations That All of Us Have to Give Up in Order to Grow.* New York: Simon & Schuster, 1986.

Wolfe, Naomi. *The Beauty Myth: How Images of Beauty Are Used Against Women,* New York: Harper Perennial, 2002.

Articles and websites that may be of interest:

Asch, Solomon E. "Opinions and Social Pressure." *Scientific American* 193 (1955): 31–35.

Carmichael, Peter A. "The Sense of Ugliness." *The Journal of Aesthetics and Art Criticism* 30, no. 4 (1972): 495–498.

Cawley, John. "Body Weight and Women's Labor Market Outcome." *NBER Working Paper* no. 7841, August 2000.

Cixous, Helene. "The Laugh of the Medusa." *Signs: Journal of Women in Culture and Society* 1, no. 4 (1976).

Crisp, Arthur H. "Dysmorphophobia and The Search for Cosmetic Surgery." *British Medical Journal* 282, no. 6270 (1981): 1099–1100.

Dull, Diana, and Candace West. "Accounting for Cosmetic Surgery: The Accomplishment of Gender." *Social Problems* 38, no. 1 (1991): 54–70.

Eileraas, Karina. "Witches, Bitches and Fluids: Girl Bands Performing Ugliness as Resistance." *The Drama Review* 41, no. 3 (1997): 122–139.

Frothingham, A. L. "Medusa, Apollo and the Great Mother." *American Journal of Archaeology* 15, no. 3 (1911): 349–377.

Greenfield, Lauren. "Kiddie Spas: The End of Innocence." *Marie Claire, UK* (May 2002): 163–168.

Hamermesh, Daniel S., and Jeff E. Biddle. "Beauty and the Labor Market." *American Economic Review, American Economic Association* 84, no. 5 (1994): 1174–94.

Hopkins, Clark. "The Sunny Side of the Greek Gorgon." *Beytus* 14 (1961): 25–35.

Holguin, Jamie. "Iran: Nose Job Capital Of World." *CBS Evening News*, CBS News, http://www.cbsnews.com/stories/2005/05/02/eveningnews/main692495.shtml (accessed May 28, 2010).

Kalick, Michael, et al. "Does Human Facial Attractiveness Honestly Advertise Health? Longitudinal Data on an Evolutionary Question." *Psychological Science* 9, no. 1 (1998): 8–13.

Kieran, Matthew. "Aesthetic Value: Beauty, Ugliness and Incoherence." *Philosophy* 72, no. 281 (1997): 383–399.

Klassen, A., et al. "Contrasting Evidence of the Effectiveness of Cosmetic Surgery from Two Health Related Quality of Life Measures." *Journal of Epidemiology and Community Health* 53, no. 7 (1999): 440–441.

Lim, Louisa. "Painful Memories for China's Footbinding Survivors." www.npr.org/templates/story/story.php?storyId=8966942 (accessed May 30, 2010).

Luscombe, Belinda. "The Truth About Teen Girls." *Time* (September 11, 2008): http://www.time.com/time/magazine/article/0,9171,1840556-2,00.html.

Ma, Xin. "Bullying and Being Bullied: To What Extent Are Bullies Also Victims?" *American Educational Research Journal* 38, no. 2 (2001): 351–370.

Martin, Mary C., and James Gentry. "Stuck in the Model Trap: The Effects of Beautiful Models in Ads on Female Pre-Adolescents and Adolescents." *Journal of Advertising* 26, no. 2 (1997): 19–34.

Mead, Rebecca. "Slim For Him." *The New Yorker* (January 15, 2001): 48.

Miller, Merry N., and Andrés J. Pumarieaga. "Culture and Eating Disorders: A Historical and Cross-Cultural Review." *Psychiatry* 64, no. 2 (2001): 93–110.

Ruel, Michael D. "Vanity Tax." *The Journal of Legal Medicine* 28, no. 1 (2007): 119–134.

Saguy, Tamar, et al. "Interacting Like a Body: Objectification Can Lead Women to Narrow Their Presence in Social Interactions." *Psychological Science* (2010): 21, No. 2. 178–182

University of North Carolina at Chapel Hill. "Three Out Of Four American Women Have Disordered Eating, Survey Suggests." *ScienceDaily* (April 23, 2008): http://www.sciencedaily.com/releases/2008/04/080422202514.htm (accessed May 30, 2010).

Vogel, Susan Mullen. "Baule Scarification: The Mark of Civilization." In *Marks of Civilization: Artistic Transformations of the Human Body*, edited by Arnold Rubin. Los Angeles: Museum of Cultural History, UCLA, 1988: 97–106.

Windermere, Arthur. "Why Are All Ugly People Evil?" http://hubpages.com/hub/OnBeauty (accessed May 30, 2010).

Zaslow, Jeffrey. "Girls and Dieting, Then and Now." *Wall Street Journal Online* (September 2, 2009): http://online.wsj.com/article/SB1000142405297020473180457438682224573170.html (accessed May 30, 2010).

ACKNOWLEDGMENTS

No book springs fully formed from a writer's mind. Every author depends on those who first explored similar topics and reported what they found, and on the encouragement, counsel, and love of others. In my case this includes my teachers and students, my psychotherapy clients, my colleagues at Empire State College, my friends, and my family.

At Health Communications, my publisher, I found instant support and encouragement from former senior vice president Tom Sand, who casually asked, "Are you working on anything?" and understood immediately the book I wanted to write. My editor at HCI, Michele Matrisciani, proved herself to be open-minded, insightful, and supportive. She knew how to ask the questions that made me a better thinker and writer. Kim Weiss, Kelly Maragni, and Lori Golden have helped get my books attention for years, when I am too shy to do this for myself. Larissa Hise Henoch and Lawna Patterson Oldfield make them into works of art. And, for the third time, HCI President Peter Vegso said "Yes" to a book that would require his support in many ways.

Of course, long before any executive or editor even knew I wanted to write *Ugly As Sin*, my agent Lydia Wills listened to me ramble about the "last acceptable prejudice" and "ugliphobia" and recognized that I had something to say. Brilliant, sensitive, and hysterically funny, Lydia proved to be a good friend as well as the perfect guide through the world of publishing. She and her colleague, Alyssa Reuben, who is always upbeat, kind, and fiercely competent, were unfailingly supportive to me and my work.

Reggie Wells, my beloved teacher and friend, will forever have my gratitude for his brave example, his unstinting encouragement, and his love. His wisdom lives in these pages along with the love and perspective given so generously by my new old family Elissa Levine, Aurora Raiten, Terra Raiten, Christian Stanfield, and Dan Kimes.

Finally, as everyone who knows me understands, I am grateful to the three great loves of my life: my husband Michael D'Antonio, who thought I was smart before I did and always helps to make me sound that way; Elizabeth, who encourages me to be as brave as she is; and Amy, who worries if I'm all right. I am.

INDEX

ABOUT THE AUTHOR

Known for her ability to present rigorous and provocative ideas with warmth and empathy, **Toni Raiten-D'Antonio** is an author, a psychotherapist in private practice, and a professor of social work at Empire State College in New York. Her previous two books, *The Velveteen Principles* and *The Velveteen Principles for Women* have inspired hundreds of thousands of readers worldwide and have been used to train professionals in such varied settings as public school systems, hospitals, rehabilitation centers, and state prisons.

A former television and stage performer, Toni is a much sought-after public speaker who has entertained, motivated, and educated college students, healthcare professionals, charitable organizations, and the New York Jets football team. Her insights into human emotions, relationships, group dynamics, and leading a life of purpose have moved audiences across the country.

Toni Raiten-D'Antonio is the mother of two daughters, and she lives with her husband Michael on Long Island. She can be contacted at www.trdantonio.com.